Black and Tired

Black and Tired

*Essays on Race, Politics, Culture,
and International Development*

ANTHONY B. BRADLEY

WIPF & STOCK · Eugene, Oregon

BLACK AND TIRED
Essays on Race, Politics, Culture, and International Development

Wipf & Stock
An Imprint of Wipf and Stock Publishers
199 W. 8th Ave., Suite 3
Eugene, OR 97401
www.wipfandstock.com

ISBN 13: 978-1-60899-596-7

Manufactured in the U.S.A.

To Thomas Sowell

Contents

Acknowledgments

THIS BOOK WOULD NOT be possible if it were not for Kris Mauren and the Rev. Robert Sirico, co-founders of the Acton Institute for the Study of Religion and Liberty in Grand Rapids, Michigan where I have been affiliated as a research fellow since 2002. The Acton Institute has provided me a platform and multiple international opportunities to speak and write about the issues discussed in this volume. My principle content and style editor has been my friend and colleague Dr. Kevin Schmeising, also a research fellow at the Acton Institute. I credit Kevin with single-handedly making me sound more intelligent and coherent than I actually am. John Couretas, Acton's communication director, has masterfully worked to add the finishing touches on these essays and to disseminate them all over the world. I would also like to thank Daniel Hay, one of my research assistants at the King's College, New York, for his editing work on this volume. The King's College continues to provide exceptionally competent students for those of us writing on the synthesis of theology and economics. Christian Amondson and the team at Wipf and Stock were very gracious to work with me on this project. Finally, Lori Nieboer deserves special recognition and thanks for her meticulous skill in editing and formatting this book.

Introduction

AN ADVANTAGE OF BEING a theologian who embraces Jesus' teaching of the kingdom is the realization that God's reconciliation of all things to Christ signifies that no part of this world lies beyond the gaze of God the Father, Son, and Holy Spirit. Every aspect of life resonates with spiritual and cosmic implications. Since 2002, I have had the honor and privilege as a theologian to reflect publicly on current events with the aim of synthesizing economics and moral theology. Contemplating life from a theological perspective is nothing new; we find such reflections throughout the entire biblical narrative, from Genesis to Revelation. What follows in this book are theological and moral reflections on some of the social issues affecting our local, national, and global communities. The topics range from hip-hop, to economic developments in Guatemala, to public school education policy, and more—all examined from a theological perspective.

These essays are a form of public theology in the sense that they wrestle with this generation's issues, bringing theology to life and demonstrating God's relevance in a metamodern world. I am thankful that these essays created ancillary opportunities for me to expound on some of my theories in the mainstream media. Edited versions, for example, appeared in newspapers like the *Detroit News* and the *Atlanta-Journal Constitution*. I have also made appearances on several national radio and television broadcasts, including National Public Radio, CNN, and Fox News.

This book explores issues of race, politics and economics, social trends in culture, international development, and trends in education by integrating the following justice principles from the Acton Institute.[1] They include the following:

(1) **Dignity of the Person**—The human person, created in the image of God, is individually unique, rational, the subject of moral agency,

1. www.acton.org.

and a co-creator. Accordingly, he possesses intrinsic value and dignity, implying certain rights and duties both for himself and other persons. These truths about the dignity of the human person are known through revelation, but they are also discernible through reason.

(2) **Social Nature of the Person**—Although persons find ultimate fulfillment only in communion with God, one essential aspect of the development of persons is our social nature and capacity to act for disinterested ends. The person is fulfilled by interacting with other persons and by participating in moral goods. There are voluntary relations of exchange, such as market transactions that realize economic value. These transactions may give rise to moral value as well. There are also voluntary relations of mutual dependence, such as promises, friendships, marriages, and the family, which are moral goods. These, too, may have other sorts of value, such as religious, economic, aesthetic, and so on.

(3) **Importance of Social Institutions**—Since persons are by nature social, various human persons develop social institutions. The institutions of civil society, especially the family, are the primary sources of a society's moral culture. These social institutions are neither created by nor derive their legitimacy from the state. The state must respect their autonomy and provide the support necessary to ensure the free and orderly operation of all social institutions in their respective spheres.

(3) **Human Action**—Human persons are by nature acting persons. Through human action, the person can actualize his potentiality by freely choosing the moral goods that fulfill his nature.

(4) **Sin**—Although human beings in their created nature are good, in their current state, they are fallen and corrupted by sin. The reality of sin makes the state necessary to restrain evil. The ubiquity of sin, however, requires that the state be limited in its power and jurisdiction. The persistent reality of sin requires that we be skeptical of all utopian "solutions" to social ills such as poverty and injustice.

(5) **Rule of Law and the Subsidiary Role of Government**—The government's primary responsibility is to promote the common good, that is, to maintain the rule of law, and to preserve basic duties and rights. The government's role is not to usurp free actions, but to minimize those conflicts that may arise when the free actions of persons and social institutions result in competing interests. The state should exercise this responsibility according to the principle of subsidiarity. This principle has two components. First, jurisdictionally broader institutions must refrain

from usurping the proper functions that should be performed by the person and institutions more immediate to him. Second, jurisdictionally broader institutions should assist individual persons and institutions more immediate to the person only when the latter cannot fulfill their proper functions.

(6) **Creation of Wealth**—Material impoverishment undermines the conditions that allow humans to flourish. The best means of reducing poverty is to protect private property rights through the rule of law. This allows people to enter into voluntary exchange circles in which to express their creative nature. Wealth is created when human beings creatively transform matter into resources. Because human beings can create wealth, economic exchange need not be a zero-sum game.

(7) **Economic Liberty**—Liberty, in a positive sense, is achieved by fulfilling one's nature as a person by freely choosing to do what one ought. Economic liberty is a species of liberty so-stated. As such, the bearer of economic liberty not only has certain rights, but also duties. An economically free person, for example, must be free to enter the market voluntarily. Hence, those who have the power to interfere with the market are duty-bound to remove any artificial barrier to entry in the market, and also to protect private and shared property rights. But the economically free person will also bear the duty to others to participate in the market as a moral agent and in accordance with moral goods. Therefore, the law must guarantee private property rights and voluntary exchange.

(8) **Economic Value**—In economic theory, economic value is subjective because its existence depends on it being felt by a subject. Economic value is the significance that a subject attaches to a thing whenever he perceives a causal connection between this thing and the satisfaction of a present, urgent want. The subject may be wrong in his value judgment by attributing value to a thing that will not or cannot satisfy his present, urgent want. The truth of economic value judgments is settled just in case that thing can satisfy the expected want. While this does not imply the realization of any other sort of value, something can have both subjective economic value and objective moral value.

(9) **Priority of Culture**—Liberty flourishes in a society supported by a moral culture that embraces the truth about the transcendent origin and destiny of the human person. This moral culture leads to harmony and to the proper ordering of society. While the various institutions

within the political, economic, and other spheres are important, the family is the primary inculcator of the moral culture in a society.

My opinions and style I owe much to the work of Thomas Sowell, one of the most cogent and lucid of American socio-economic analysts. I learned from Sowell the importance of supporting my propositions with incontrovertible evidence and irrefutable facts. I am indebted also to Cornel West, whose brilliant work heavily influences and tempers my writing. Cornell West sustains an undercurrent of compassion and love in his reflections, a reminder to me that these issues are not merely academic abstractions but real concerns that affect the lives of real people. As my writing and understanding continue to grow and mature, I recognize that I do not represent "the last word" on any of these issues. I hope, however, that the following essays will advance national and international conversations about the common good and make the world, in some small measure, a better place.

PART ONE

Race

HUMAN DIGNITY, DARK SKIN, AND NEGRO DIALECT

BLACK HISTORY MONTH, A time to reflect on milestones, should also be a time to survey the road ahead and the journey yet unfinished. Why does the black underclass still struggle years after the civil-rights movement? Almost fifty years ago, Martin Luther King dreamed of a country that would value all of its men, women, and children, an America that would respect each of its citizens, regardless of skin color. Sadly, the civil rights movement and the dream of equal dignity lost focus and momentum, derailed by the pursuit of political power and "bling." The goal of racial equality, measured by statistics and achieved through government mandates, overshadowed the crusade for true solidarity, for a unified belief in the innate dignity of all human beings.

Beginning in the 1980s, many civil-rights leaders began to equate justice with socioeconomic status, focusing on how much "stuff" blacks lacked compared to whites—size of homes, college degrees, income disparities, law school admissions rates, loan approvals, and the like—instead of whether or not blacks experienced parity in the American social structure. Unfortunately, equal treatment in the eyes of society and the legal system may yield surprising results; nonetheless, equal legal and social treatment remains a better measure of justice, rather than the superficial results obtained by creative governmental coercion.

When Democratic Senator Harry Reid spoke the truth about President Obama as electable because he neither had "dark skin" nor used "negro dialect," he prophetically signaled that Americans still struggle to embrace the dignity of blacks. Reid's comments exposed what many know but would not publically confess: namely, that a combination of

1

dark skin and "negro dialect" is less than desirable and impede one's prospects for social and economic mobility. After all, some would ask, are not the stereotypical dark-skinned folks (those with substandard English skills and illegitimate children) dropping out of high school, crowding America's prison system, murdering each other, and producing materialistic and misogynistic rap music?

Civil-rights leaders would do well to resume fighting for black dignity in order to foster respect for dark skin and to encourage the use of standard English. Theologian Nonna Harrison in her 2008 essay, "The Human Person," offers a clear framework for unlocking human dignity by stressing human freedom, responsibility, love for neighbor, excellence of character, stewardship of creation, and human rationality. Imagine an America where resurgent civil-rights leaders worked to create conditions supporting a life-long process of formation and transformation of citizens who know and love their neighbors, regardless of race or class. Imagine a resurgence of dignity that orders unruly passions, impulses, and reason to excel in moral character. Imagine a resurgence of good stewardship to the status of the social norm. Imagine a resurgence that promotes sustaining human life in terms of what is good for nature and human society—a resurgence committed to cultivating practical reason, creativity in the arts and sciences, economics, politics, business, and culture.

A movement dedicated to fostering dignity instead of self-sabotaging behavior would positively spill over everywhere, from homes to schools, from streets to the criminal justice system. For example, if freedom, responsibility, and dignity became the new platform for the "advancement of colored people," black marriage rates might revert to their 1950s levels, when the percentages of white and African-American women who were currently married were roughly equal (67 and 64 per cent, respectively). Emphasizing practical reason would promote education—not sports and entertainment—as the "ticket" out of "da hood." Imagine an America where being a black man meant being a morally formed, educated "brutha," ready to contribute to improving the world.

Decades ago, when the black community revolved around the black church, these values descended from generation to generation. Today, in an era when "justice" means obsession with redistributing wealth rather than restoring dignity, character formation means nothing. Disadvantaged blacks, generationally doomed, wait for the acknowledgement that social mobility for the "dark skinned" speakers of "negro dialect" flows from the expansion of dignity and freedom, not from pursing the siren songs of riches and power.

RACE ALARMISTS HIJACK BLACK HISTORY MONTH

Black History Month must seem like Christmas for race alarmists. It presents the perfect time to unwrap statistics from racial disparity studies to imply some sort of institutional racism.

A recent example is a study titled, "Reviving the Goal of an Integrated Society: A 21st Century Challenge, by the Civil-Rights Project at UCLA." The authors call on the Obama administration to take action against "resegregation." The report sounds the alarm that "40 percent of Latinos and 39 percent of blacks now attend intensely segregated schools. The average black and Latino student is now in a school that has nearly 60 percent of students from families who are near or below the poverty line."

High concentrations of blacks and Latinos pose a problem for critics who believe the myth that blacks and Latinos need white influence to achieve academic success. It is the New Racism: the concept that minorities cannot survive without whites. The report additionally confuses race with class. What ultimately matters is not that blacks and Latinos attend minority schools but that lower-income black and Latino parents sadly lack the freedom to send their children to whatever school will best educate them, a freedom exercised by many in higher income brackets, including middle-class minorities.

As a factor in low academic achievement scores, a predominantly black and Latino student demographic proves irrelevant. All black schools have produced high achieving students in the past. Thomas Sowell tells of a segregated high school that, from 1870 to 1955, repeatedly equaled or exceeded national norms on standardized tests. During its eighty-five years in existence, the majority of Washington's M Street/ Dunbar High School's 12,000 graduates went on to higher education, an unusual achievement for any school—white or black—during this era. Moreover, many of the M Street/Dunbar School graduates attended Harvard and other elite colleges in the early twentieth century.

Sowell notes that, as of 1916, nine black students from the entire country attended Amherst College, six of whom came from the M Street/ Dunbar School. During the period from 1918 to 1923, the school's graduates went on to earn twenty-five degrees from the Ivy League colleges

Amherst, Williams, and Wesleyan. The first graduating blacks from West Point and Annapolis hailed from M Street/Dunbar, as did the first black full professor at a major university, the first black federal judge, the first black general, the first black Cabinet member, and the first black elected to the United States Senate since Reconstruction.

Segregated schools produced such notables as Mary McLeod Bethune, Thurgood Marshall, and Martin Luther King, Jr. The belief that racial diversity is the key to academic success has no empirical basis. If this myth were true, explaining academic success in more mono-racial societies such as Japan, Germany, and the Netherlands would be difficult. Devotees of the new racism cannot fathom black and Latino success without whites nearby, but the real problem is that black and Latino children lack educational options consonant with their dignity and potential.

Given the current achievement disparities between the middle class disadvantaged and the regardless of race, can social engineering be more important than increasing performance in lower income neighborhoods? Solutions for difficult lower income situations are beyond President Obama's scope, for morally based problems require morally based solutions.

A prime example is the relationship between academic achievement and family structure. According to a Heritage Foundation study, children aged three to twelve from families with married, biological parents, performed, on average, better on a mathematical calculation test than did their peers from families with a biological mother and a stepfather, families with an unmarried biological mother and a cohabiting partner, or families with a biological father only. This study, one in a multitude of data, illustrates the influence of family character on academic accomplishment.

Nor can Obama's administration do anything about the fact that free people choose to live in neighborhoods where they share similar income and values, regardless of race. The black and Latino middle-class do not live in "da hood" either. When choosing where to live, free people use different criteria than the elite, and thus live in different areas than the elite would prefer. Any alternative proposed by government planners, as demonstrated by the abysmal failure of school busing programs, usually makes matters worse.

What is best for low-income black and Latino students is what is best for all students: stable and supportive families, parental options, and high achieving schools with stellar teachers. These require local solutions that have nothing to do with shoddy "disparity" studies and the New Racism currently promoted in Washington.

THE ENDURING FOOLISHNESS OF RACIAL POLITICS

With only a few weeks to Election Day, racial politics has reared its pathetic head as pundits attempt to decipher poll numbers and audience comments at political rallies. It seems silly that adults in America may vote along racial lines but it should come as no surprise. Many *people* on the ideological margins of society vote irrationally. In fact, voting along racial lines says less about racism than it does about the lack of mature civic responsibility among voters indifferent to the nation's common good.

When used as the ultimate criterion for supporting or rejecting a candidate, playing the race card is both indefensible and shallow—a trade-off, however, for freedom of choice. Exercising true freedom of choice entails a grave responsibility. One should consider a candidate's position on important issues, such as abortion, the role of government in meeting the needs of the poor, foreign policy, and education. Living in a democracy that affords its citizens real liberty, rather than under a dictatorship's regime, should make grateful Americans responsibly exercise their privilege to vote for their candidates of choice, a choice based upon more than skin color.

When African Americans, Latinos, and Asians lament, "It's 2008 and racism still exists in America," the temptation is to shout, "What fairytale were you reading that said racism would ever cease?" An historic tenet of Judeo-Christianity, along with many other religions, is that evil exists in the world. As long as people lack the moral development to escape it, there will always be racism.

What is most alarming about the media's recent displays of racial politics is that many American voters do not possess the civic virtue to put their personal racial views aside for the sake of what is best for the nation. Race does not determine a person's position on issues. Do Maxine Waters and Condoleezza Rice think alike simply because they are both black women? Shallow voting is the art of the imperceptive.

In light of the monumental problems facing the nation—the Middle East conflicts, the American banking crisis, transitions in energy use , new alliances among socialist regimes in Europe, Latin America, and Asia, and the complex issues in Africa—the United States should cringe when the rest of the world observes Americans reducing the presidential election to race and gender.

Americans must embrace their responsibility as virtuous citizens concerned about the common good. This means disregarding non-essential issues like race and choosing a candidate with the character and competence necessary to offer leadership on pressing current issues.

For example, which candidate demonstrates the wisdom to promote free market economics, historically the best method of creating wealth and lifting people out of poverty? Which candidate champions justice embedded in a rule of law that keeps corruption, power, and greed in check?

Which candidate has the humility to know that neither he, nor any other small group of central planners, has enough knowledge or expertise to use government to manage the lives of 300 million people? Which candidate has the courage to fight for human life? Which candidate has the personal integrity to encourage trust and cooperation? In light of these critical questions, who cares about the candidate's race?

The term "Bradley Effect" (after 1980s California gubernatorial candidate Tom Bradley) describes the phenomenon whereby white voters actually cast ballots for white instead of black candidates in greater numbers than earlier polls indicate. As November approaches, questions surrounding a potential Bradley Effect pale in comparison to the possibility that many people will vote according to irrational criteria in general, the potential "foolishness effect."

May truth and reason prevail in the coming weeks, so that both campaigns and the media will keep in front of voters the candidates' principles and policies—rather than talking points befitting high school yearbook senior superlatives.

A NEW VISION FOR AMERICA'S BLACK MEN

Tens of thousands of black St. Louis residents gathered at the June 1 "Call to Oneness March" to protest against the rampant crime that continues to shackle generations to nihilism and self-destruction. An estimated 50,000 people marched. However, today the question remains, "now what?" The call for black men to embrace "individual responsibility" without defining "responsibility" makes matters worse. Black men need a more radical call to go beyond the individual self and demonstrate some concern for others.

As of last Thursday, St. Louis had 61 homicides so far this year, fifteen more than the same period last year. Of that swelling number, at least 43 victims were black males, according to the St. Louis American, the city's black newspaper. One hundred thirty-eight homicides last year makes St. Louis one of the most dangerous cities in America.

While the Gateway City's problems appear to be especially severe, they are not unique. Across America, black people long for a magic solution, for the next black messiah to come and unite "the community." He is not coming. No single variable will solve this crisis. Confronting the issues of morality, education, family, marriage, job creation, and music complicate any solution matrix. At the heart of any solution, however, must be a move toward responsible service. Marching up and down every black neighborhood in America will change nothing until people hear the radical call sounded.

Previous calls for "individual responsibility" without virtue bred the kind of selfishness summarized in the phrase, "I'm gon' get mine!" In many black communities, civil war rages. To tell black males to focus on "individual responsibility" stops neither the violence nor the fatherlessness.

In fact, radical individualism allows one, with a clear conscience, to murder one's neighbor or impregnate women to whom there is no intention of remaining faithfully committed. The black community does not simply want individually responsible black men: it wants black men who see that they exist for the service of others.

A different vision for men, according to former NFL player Joe Ehrmann in *Season of Life,* must start with black men declaring war against false masculinity predicated on sexual conquests, material possessions, and physical dominance over others. Black men must foster personal relationships that affirm their strength to family members, friends, neighbors, and co-workers. Black men must move beyond the base selfishness of "gettin' mine" or "gettin' paid." They must selflessly accept accountability for all of their actions, private and public, and acknowledge their impact on the world. Black men must draw upon their strengths and talents to improve the world and wage war against injustice. Ultimately, black men must develop empathy for the plight of others.

Until black men embrace a new vision—being a real man means existing to serve others—the self-sabotage will continue. The black religious community historically has played the leading role in forming those virtues that foster a vocation of responsible service, but today the church is impotent, its credibility among with the hip-hop generation washed away in the currents of contemporary culture.

"Individual responsibility" means nothing if is not directed at cultivating the virtue necessary to make a positive contribution to the lives of others. Prior to the civil-rights movement, looking out for each other was endemic, partly a function of necessity. Those values were lost in a single generation. What must be next for St. Louis, and other cities where blacks are destroying each other, is a multi-faceted approach that casts a new vision for making a contribution rather than retribution.

There is no more fulfilling human vocation than to know that one is making a positive difference in the world, no matter how big or small. What matters, in the end, is not that one assumes responsibility for oneself but that one shares in the responsibility for others.

BILL COSBY IS RIGHT, AGAIN

Bill Cosby cements his role as America's sage social critic with the release of his new book, *Come On People: On The Path From Victims to Victors.* Co-authored with Dr. Alvin Poussaint of Harvard Medical School, *Come On People* clearly explains that black America's hope for escape from abysmal self-destruction is moral formation—not government programs or blaming white people.

This book will arouse needed controversy as it challenges the victim mentality often promulgated by men like Jesse Jackson, Al Sharpton, Michael Eric Dyson, and other black liberal elites. Cosby and Poussaint are direct, candid, and engender a spirit of urgency. Putting silly racial politics aside, black America needs to concentrate on the real reasons it is hemorrhaging.

Cosby and Poussaint open with the $64,000 question: "What's Going On With Black Men?" Without strong black men, they argue, the black community will continue to decompose. In 1950, five out of every six black children were born into a two-parent family; today, that number is less than two out of six. Irresponsible men and fatherlessness have destroyed for many black Americans any hope of achieving Dr. King's dream. White people do not make black men father children outside of marriage.

"A house without a father is a challenge. A neighborhood without fathers is a catastrophe," the authors note. Many black boys never mature morally into manhood because they lack the guidance of virtuous men. Many of these young black men, left to their own devices, fall into criminal activities and consequently serve time in jail. The perpetrators in ninety-four percent of all black murders are other blacks. Visiting a Klu Klux Klan rally would seem safer to some blacks than living in their own neighborhoods.

Blaming white people for personal irresponsibility is laughable. "For all the talk of systemic racism and government screw-ups," Cosby and Poussaint insist, "we [blacks] must look to ourselves and understand our responsibility." No government program, well-meaning white liberal patronization, guilt-driven Saturday morning urban mission project, or large sum of unearned cash assistance will overcome the challenge: blacks need to step up, reject the materialistic, narcissistic American Dream and love their neighborhoods again.

The book also emphasizes the centrality of the family. Children need a mother and a father, and, in turn, women and children need men. The authors brilliantly highlight the fact that many black children are lazy and addicted to television. They speak substandard English. They doubt their dignity and worth. Some children suffer sexual and physical abuse because they lack loving homes headed by strong men serving their wives and children.

Placing a high value on education had been a pillar of the black community until recently, when the minds of many black youths began to be crammed with the "self-defeating, self-degrading, and finally self-destructive" music that perverts virtue. Black children fail in school because many black parents drop the ball, for various difficult reasons. Instead of spending time reading books, the children park themselves in front of the television set and soak up all that BET offers—the good and the bad.

Cosby's book challenges blacks to care about their own health, in light of chronic obesity, Type II diabetes, and the HIV/AIDS crisis. It encourages blacks to overcome the stigma of counseling and to seek help for the scars from past physical, sexual, and emotional abuse.

Cosby and Poussaint conclude their pleading with a call to self-efficacy: one's belief about personal capacity to contribute to the good and exercise influence over events that affect one's life. "If you are not working and your only job is to stand in line so that the government can sustain you, then you are not contributing to your community," they write.

In the end, black America is called to renew the principles, ideals, and institutions that have carried blacks along since slavery: faith in God, sustained marriages and family, an emphasis on learning, prudent financial empowerment, building community, and an unwavering hope that the future will be better for their children and grandchildren.

Not all of the book's proposals conform to Christian standards—their allowance of "committed partnerships" in lieu of an exclusive focus on lifelong marriage, for example. Nevertheless, Cosby and Poussaint send a clear, cogent message: only individual blacks bestowing lives of virtue on the next generation, one child at a time, can achieve moral and economic success in the black community.

BLACK VIRTUE: SUCCESS BEYOND THE SUPER BOWL

Deciding which team to cheer for in the Super Bowl usually poses no problem for most black people. Many black Americans are raised to cheer for NFL teams with black coaches or black quarterbacks—no matter what.

With two black coaches squaring off in Super Bowl XLI, black Americans discovered they were free to care about the game itself rather than how it furthered the civil-rights movement agenda. It took forty-one years, but America finally bore witness to the universal truth that, in a context of freedom, hard work and moral character contain more promise than racial entitlement.

Even with the NFL's "Rooney Rule" (adopted in 2002) requiring any team engaged in hiring a head coach to assemble a racially diverse candidate slate, one can still make the case that government-coerced affirmative action would not have been necessary in the NFL. Neither Tony Dungy nor Lovie Smith actually needed the program. A decade ago——before Rooney—Dungy became head coach of the Tampa Bay franchise, and hired Lovie Smith as an assistant coach; they coached together there from 1996–2000.

Nearly 70 percent of NFL players this season and 22 percent of the head coaches are black—an achievement to celebrate. These percentages actually exceed the percentage of blacks in America as a whole, meaning blacks in the NFL now fare better than they would if the league were operated under government-mandated quotas based on population statistics (blacks comprise 13 percent of the U.S. population).

The NFL is not necessarily a model of racial virtue. It has admittedly been slow to diversify, repeatedly passing over good black assistant coaches for head coaching positions. Yet, in recent history, a few risk-taking franchise owners, without coercion from the government, freely hired black coaches such as Art Shell and Dennis Green. They believed and demonstrated a strong lesson drawn from economics: the best employees produce the best results regardless of race.

Tony Dungy has taken this economic lesson to a new level by being a major mentor of quality black coaches. Four Dungy assistants have gone on to head coaching positions, the most recent being 34-year-old Mike Tomlin, hired by the Pittsburgh Steelers as that team's first black head coach.

In the end, it was hard work and moral character in a context of freedom and risk that catapulted Dungy, now leading the Indianapolis Colts, and Smith, currently with the Bears in Chicago, to the Super Bowl. It is good for black boys in America to see how being a grown-up man of virtue opens up opportunities to lead $700 million dollar football teams to the Super Bowl.

However, while many blacks hoped that their sons watched this year's Super Bowl imagining that one day they, too, could be an NFL football coach, it is important to remember that blacks can become doctors and lawyers far more easily than they can become NFL coaches. The success of Dungy and Smith pales by the fact that most black high school football players will never play college football, professional football, or be head coaches. Black boys need to know that there are twelve times as many jobs for blacks in law and medicine as there are in sports.

To build a successful career—whether in football, law, or medicine—one must lay a solid foundation of moral character. This success is almost impossible to achieve in the midst of the self-sabotaging lifestyles lived out among so many blacks: the almost 5 percent incarceration rate, the 9.2 percent unemployment rate, the 11.8 percent high school drop-out rate, or the 69.3 percent of births blacks cause outside of marriage.

Dungy and Smith, by their calm attitudes and outspoken Christian faith, display the rewards of virtue.

"I'm proud to be the first African-American coach to win this," Dungy said after the game. "But again, more than anything, Lovie Smith and I are not only African-American but also Christian coaches, showing you can do it the Lord's way. We're more proud of that."

The moral of this year's historic Super Bowl extends beyond racial boundaries: In a free society, the virtues of hard work and moral character are the best keys to success.

DOES BLACK HISTORY HAVE A FUTURE?

For many, black history month means the celebration of American blacks' progress since the 1950s. However, two aspects of pre-civil rights-era black history—strong men and strong families—must reemerge to ensure the future of black history. The current crisis of masculinity, marriage, family, education, and moral formation among many blacks demands immediate attention before more generations fall through the cracks.

An ancient fact of human civilization is that marriage and family serve as key pillars of civil society. In the black community, as in much of America, the idea of marriage is dying. The latest census figures show that by age thirty-four, 41.5 percent of black men remain single compared to 24.9 percent for Asians, 28.2 percent for Hispanics, and 28.1 percent for whites. This fact is set against the unsurprising finding, reported in a 2005 report by the Institute for American Values, "that marriage clearly appears to promote the economic, social, familial, and psychological well-being of African American men and women."

In addition, HIV/AIDS and abortion continually threaten black life in America. In this era, 43 percent of all black pregnancies end in abortion, and, according to a February 2006 Black AIDS Institute report, of the estimated 1.3 million Americans living with HIV/AIDS, nearly half of them are black. Sadly, between 2000 and 2003, blacks were 51 percent of new HIV diagnoses followed by whites at 32 percent and Hispanics at 15 percent.

Tragically, more black men pass through the criminal justice system than through America's college and university system. In Baltimore, for example, 52 percent of black men in their twenties are in jail, on parole, or on probation. Imagine, instead, what type of city Baltimore would be if 52 percent of black males were college graduates or in college or graduate school?

Additionally, Historically Black Colleges and Universities (HBCUs) now primarily educate black women, with the female to male ratios at most schools approaching two to one. Howard University's female population, for example, is 64 percent of its student body; Hampton University's is 61 percent; Florida A&M's is 57 percent.

In 1985, Leanne Payne wrote a provocative book called *Crisis in Masculinity*, which applies to black men now more than ever. The sources of the crisis are many: welfare programs' encouragement of broken families and irresponsibility; the post-1960s declining influence of the black church; the emasculating agenda of black feminism; and the addictions of materialism, consumerism, anti-intellectualism, and radical individualism. Consequently, the possibility looms that only the black elite will progress, leaving the rest behind, enslaved to dependency or incarceration.

Black feminists, such as Bell Hooks in *We Real Cool: Black Men and Masculinity*, continue to spew the pathetic myth that much of the impending demise of the black male results from "imperialist white-supremacist capitalist patriarchy." In Hook's vision, true masculinity has little to do with righteous male leadership in the home. "I don't need a man" is the feminist mantra that creates a context wherein generations of black male youth go unfathered, unchurched, unprotected from abuse, and left to be raised by law enforcement or the foster care system.

Hooks does not trust the traditional black church, bemoans male aggression, and disdains the free market (even though she makes a living in the market, selling books and lecturing). The solutions to the present crisis, however, begin precisely in those areas Hooks rejects. If black men returned to the black church that has served as the backbone of black people since slavery, and adopted the brilliant and economically liberating "Declaration of Financial Empowerment" developed by *Black Enterprise Magazine*, for example, it would change America forever.

Caricatured black male aggression is not a problem requiring resolution, but rather a powerful trait needing direction toward its destiny in love. Wherever black males are lovingly raised to fight aggressively for what is true, noble, pure, and admirable, one finds great marriages, stable families, a love for learning, moral formation, economic wisdom, and a platform of empowerment able to catapult black America beyond Martin Luther King's dream.

KING'S DREAM: BEYOND BLACK AND WHITE

Dr. Martin Luther King Jr., dreamed of a day when society would not judge blacks by the color of their skin. Yet many Americans remain incapable of anything other than racial reasoning. Income disparities, housing disparities, healthcare disparities, and education disparities are defined by race, as though racial distinctions define some sort of single-celled organism—not complex human beings. Society must pay less attention to the white/black conflict and focus instead on restoring the freedom and dignity of all people, just as King desired.

Many black commentators protest that Americans laud everything "white" as normal, yet many blacks still use whites as the measuring stick for black progress. Who cares how well blacks live as compared to whites? Does it really matter? In fact, the greatest impediment to appropriating King's dream is the unwillingness to move beyond a white social barometer.

In all truth, equal achievement to whites still leaves blacks lagging behind Asian Americans and Hispanics in many areas. Why should the whites' achievement status serve as the norm for blacks, when whites, as a group, do not produce the nation's best?

For example, Asian Americans (who have now fallen victim to the label homogenous) far exceed whites on multiple achievement fronts. As the fastest growing ethnic group in the nation, 60 percent of Asian Americans earn $50,000 or more annually compared to whites at 54 percent and blacks at 32 percent, according to the U.S. Census Bureau. Moreover, the median Asian American family income is nearly $6,000 more than whites and over $27,000 more than that of blacks.

In educational achievement, 2005 Census Bureau data reveal that 49.4 percent of Asian Americans possess at least a college degree, compared to whites at 28.2 percent, and blacks at 17.6 percent. Consequently, Asians enjoy the lowest unemployment rates of all ethnic groups in America, including whites, at 3.8 percent. The College Board reports that in 2005, Asian American students scored not only the highest mean SAT scores, but also those Asian American seniors earned the highest mean GPAs among all students nationally that year. Even more telling was the discovery that in 2005, blacks trailed Native Americans, Asian Americans, Mexican Americans, and Puerto Ricans in mean SAT scores and GPAs.

If blacks trail all people of color in educational achievement, why focus on the black/white achievement gap? A 2001 Rand Corporation study rightly concludes, that "although white Americans are often used as a yardstick for measuring progress of other ethnic populations, in many respects they are far from an ideal population." Better solutions question why black students trail all broad ethnic groups in SAT performance.

Assuming an international perspective also aids in looking beyond the black/white conflict. In the international marketplace, what matters most is not how blacks compare to whites but how Americans, regardless of race, compare to the rest of the world. The National Center for Education Statistics in 2003 reported that American eighth graders perform worse in science than do eighth graders from Australia, China, Estonia, Hungary, Japan, Korea, Scotland, The Netherlands, and more. Additionally, American eighth graders score significantly in science than do their peers from Australia, Belgium, China, Italy, Japan, Korea, Latvia, Malaysia, the Netherlands, Russia, Singapore, and the Slovak Republic.

International comparisons provide valuable information to enrich the common goals for all Americans. Skin color assessments, on the contrary, divide and distract from the common mission to provide all Americans with equal opportunities to prosper freely.

In his 1967 speech "Where Do We Go from Here," King again dreams of an America where no one shouts "white power" or "black power," but "everybody talks about God's power and human power." Only by moving beyond racial reasoning will King's dream to make America a great nation come to fruition by inviting blacks into their international destiny as people of dignity and liberty.

ROSA PARKS AND THE TWO BLACK AMERICAS

On December 1, 1955, Rosa Parks defied government control and chose her own seat on a bus. Her exercise of liberty, that seminal decision to sit at the front of the bus, launched the civil-rights movement. Rosa Parks changed America forever.

In the following decades, Rosa Parks witnessed the emergence of two black Americas: one enjoying the freedom to work and thrive, and one trapped in the net of government-administered welfare. Black America is demarcated between those free to make their own choices and those whose choices are made for them by government—the latter being the very oppression that Parks, Martin Luther King, and others fought against.

Parks witnessed decades of mixed black progress. For example, today more than 40 percent of all blacks freely live in America's suburbs, while 20 percent live in the so-called "inner city." In 2001, one black America had a median two-parent family income of $60,693, while the 20.7 percent in another other black America remained below the poverty line. There are more than 1.4 million African American households with annual incomes of $75,000 or more, while 40 percent of all blacks make less than $25,000 per year.

In terms of education, 17.6 percent of blacks earn college degrees compared to 49.4 percent of Asians (only 30.6 percent of whites have degrees). Unfortunately, low standard public schools shackle a large segment of black America, sabotaging their children's futures in a global economy. In Wisconsin public schools, only 41 percent of blacks graduate from high school. Conversely, some black parents can afford to send their children to predominantly white private schools or to prestigious all-black private schools like the Romar Academy in the suburbs of Atlanta.

Economically disadvantaged blacks, trapped in welfare programs, languished behind from this federalized dehumanization. The welfare bureaucracy controlled the poor's housing choices, ensnared them in sub-standard schools, limited medical care, and crimped personal savings. More affluent and self-supporting black Americans, however, remained freely connected to foundational institutions that have always helped blacks prosper regardless of the political climate.

Public assistance keeps people from leading independent lives over time. Dependency on government deadens the human spirit. When people earn their own money, and use it to provide for themselves and their dependents, they derive a sense of autonomy, self-worth, and personal responsibility that is denied them by welfare.

The crusade Rosa Parks' inspired succeeded because it was morally justified. Discrimination against black workers, voters, and homebuyers was unjust and a violation of the inherent dignity of all human beings. Nevertheless, Rosa Parks survived to witness government absolve poor blacks of the moral and economic responsibilities required of everyone. Rosa Parks witnessed the abortion rate among black women skyrocket to 43 percent, public housing turn into violent, drug-ridden neighborhoods, and the dignity of blacks damaged by men who, with tacit government approval, abandon all responsibility for their own children. In 1950, single women headed only 18 percent of black families; today that number totals more than 45 percent. Rosa Parks witnessed the poor black's attitude shift from feeling stigmatized by welfare to accepting welfare as a birthright.

Worst of all, Rosa Parks witnessed one of the worst methodological mistakes arising from the 1960s—namely, looking to government and politics as the primary means of social mobility. Historically, the most politically and economically powerful minority groups in the United States are those least enmeshed in politics. For example, Asians in America rarely run for office, yet they surpass all racial groups in terms of income and education attainment. In 2004, the poverty rate declined for Asians (9.8 percent in 2004, down from 11.8 percent in 2003) and remained unchanged for blacks (24.7 percent).

The black America that focuses on financial independence, entrepreneurship, education, and a renaissance of black pastoral leadership will remain primarily outside of government control. Truly liberated blacks are those free to make their own morally formed choices without government involvement. To continue Parks' legacy is to free blacks disempowered by government surrogacy. Restoring black independence and. black dignity, therefore, requires a resurgence of black religious leadership, a focus on education, and a renewal of marriage and family. These pillars of the civil-rights movement stand intact as the architecture for the true liberation of blacks left behind.

CREATING BLACK HISTORY

When Carter G. Woodson established Black History Week in 1926 (later changed to Black History Month in 1976) to honor past black accomplishments, he had no idea that the future of black achievement could be so threatened. When the extraordinary potential of blacks falls short of real achievement, should this be a surprise? Substandard education, poor health care choices, and genocidal abortion rates conspire to stifle the intellectual and creative potential of many blacks. In an independent, moral black society, these same people would realize their full God given potential; they would use their amazing talents to change the world. Past leaders such as Martin Luther King believed that God created blacks for more than self-destruction. These past leaders desired freedom so that blacks could live according to the dignity inherent in them as children of God.

The leading causes of death for black Americans are heart disease, cancer, stroke, and diabetes. With the exception of cancer, there is much evidence to suggest links between these diseases and poor diets. According to Dr. Michael Bradley, Assistant Professor of Pharmacy Practice at University of Arkansas for Medical Sciences, quality health care in the black community has to do with "people making better food choices." These choices are difficult to make with the fast-food saturation in minority communities. In New Orleans, for example, predominantly black neighborhoods have 2.4 fast food restaurants per square mile compared to 1.5 square miles for white neighborhoods.

Fast-food restaurants cater to the unhealthy food choices of blacks in these neighborhoods—it is the principle of supply and demand. If blacks did not want food mired in saturated fats and loaded with calories and sodium, or sucrose-laden beverages, fast-food restaurants would change their menus to include healthier choices. The nearly suicidal causal chain of unhealthy food choices, obesity, Type II diabetes, heart disease, and stroke can be broken. Unless blacks and other Americans exercise better, educated choices, they fail in the stewardship of their bodies and erode the necessary foundation of good health upon which to build communities of work, creativity, and prosperity.

Educational failure poses another problem compromising the promise of a better future. Jay Greene, Senior Fellow at the Manhattan Institute, reports that nationally only 56 percent of blacks graduate from high school. Of all black students who stay in school, around 75 percent score lower on standardized tests than comparably situated whites, according to the Brookings Institution. These low scores guarantee that many blacks will never escape the nation's service sector, unemployment, or the welfare rolls. In the age of information and technology, uneducated and poorly educated blacks struggle to overcome this disadvantage, handicapped at the outset from making significant, historical contributions.

Finally, abortion ravages the black community at rates worse than slavery or Jim Crow ever did. According to the Allan Gutmacher Institute, over 43 percent of all black pregnancies end in abortion. Although blacks represent only 12 percent of the American population, they account for almost 35 percent of all abortions. Since 1973, over 13 million blacks have fallen victim to abortion. Blacks in America are disappearing.

What is most bizarre about these numbers is that the so-called "black leadership" remains silent. In other contexts, these statistics would warrant the charge of "racism." In Mississippi alone, 73 percent of all of the state's abortions are by black women. Where are the NAACP and Congressional Black Caucus? If 73 percent of Mississippi blacks were not graduating from high school, the Rainbow Coalition would organize a "March on Washington." Is Planned Parenthood guilty of "racial profiling" for locating 71 percent of its facilities in minority communities? God created blacks with the potential to make history. Black women, in continuing to abort their unborn children, also destroy the potential to change and shape history. If black lives end before they have a chance to begin, how can change occur?

The choices black people make threaten the creation of black history far more than white people's actions or "the system." Some black youths drop out of high school by choice; others remain trapped in substandard schools by government edict, even though minority parents desperately want freedom to choose the best schools. Consuming unhealthy, poisonous diets, and thereby increasing the known risks of terminal diseases, is a choice. Irresponsible sexual behavior relying on abortion as contraception is likewise a destructive decision.

In order for Black History Month to include blacks beyond Martin Luther King, blacks need the opportunity to live, live well, and learn enough to meet the critical needs of the world. The book of Proverbs says, "There is a way that seems right to a man but in the end it leads to death." Poor levels of education, unhealthy diets, and abortion may seem permissible to some, but these things slowly lead to the death of black history.

BEYOND BLACK HISTORY

Every February in classrooms, school assemblies, and church programs all over America, a spotlight illuminates many achievements of African Americans. These triumphant achievements, made in the face of oppression, segregation, and discrimination, deserve recognition. Unfortunately—as the current presidential election cycle highlights—many political leaders and intellectuals still act as though the black past is the black present, as though the pernicious circumstances of history still oppress the present.

Fueled by three related misconceptions, this backwards thinking prevents blacks from moving forward.

First, even though the black church is no longer the force that it once was in black communities, politicians still think it necessary to offer words from pulpits. Their intention, of course, is not to preach the Gospel but to offer rhetoric about their concern for "the black community." Although currently ineffective, the tactic arises from the historically pivotal role of the black church. From the time of slavery through the civil-rights movement, the church was the most influential institution among black people. Black pastors served as mediators between various black communities and the white world.

In addition, prior to the civil-rights movement, white politicians, businessmen, and other leaders would request meetings with local black clergy to discuss significant issues. These pastors would then return to their respective congregations and report the substance of the meetings. The importance of this mediating role for the clergy declined with the onset of the civil rights movement, as more blacks benefited from economic and social progress and gained direct access to realms previously reserved for black leaders.

One result of this progress is a rise in blacks' economic prowess. Black spending power, estimated at $630 billion annually, remains unrecognized. Politicians genuinely solicitous of blacks' interests should make appearances at this year's Black Enterprise Conference or at various chapters of 100 Black Men Inc., a national youth mentoring organization committed to the intellectual development and economic empowerment of the African-American community based upon respect for family, spirituality, justice and integrity.

Something less auspicious also contributes to the decline of the black clergy's influence: most black Americans no longer attend church. Sadly, as the black clergy's leadership role has declined, it has also been distorted. Many black pastors allow their churches to be pawns in a political chess match. For many politicians in both parties, black pastors and their congregations serve as a means to win elections, a fact made painfully obvious in the months following presidential inaugurations. For example, the promised war on poverty, in the end, destroyed many black urban neighborhoods.

Second, it is finally time to put to death the idea that black people have or need "a black leader." Blacks no longer need designated leaders. Like whites, Asians, or any other group of individuals, blacks are capable of thinking on their own. Who are the leaders of the Asian community or the white community? These questions should sound just as ridiculous when applied to blacks in America. The idea that black America needs another Martin Luther King, Jr. archetype is excess baggage from a bygone time. Both Jesse Jackson and Al Sharpton have been categorically—and rightly—rejected in their attempts to claim the coveted title "Leader of the Black Community."

Blacks are mainstream Americans. Blacks do not need national leaders because the struggle for equality under the law successfully provided opportunity to enter America's institutions at all levels. Blacks now possess the freedom to exercise the same liberties that the rest of Americans enjoy and in the same manner—including the right to life, liberty, and pursuit of happiness.

Third, the idea that an entity meaningfully called "the black community" needs to be challenged as well. Blacks in America are by no means homogenous; they occupy diverse places in both the geographical and socio-economic landscapes. Forty percent of blacks live in America's suburbs, while only about one-fifth live in urban centers. Blacks do not share the same values or religion. Although various "black communities" may exist, the idea that one needs to reach out to "the" black community is nothing more than resurrected Jim Crow rhetoric. Referring to issues in "the black community" actually means referring to nothing substantial, merely a spectrum of issues that concern other Americans as well.

Overall, the lingering notion persists that the so-called black community needs individual black leaders—that this separate black community matters because racism still exists. Some view black progress only in terms of white racism. Blacks have not made much progress, this line of argument reasons, because racism still exists. Of course, racism still exists. Racism is a sin and, as long as people sin, racism will exist. This is not to say that one should not fight against racism, just as one should challenge all evil. Blacks must expose racism's irrationality, an irrationality rooted in ignorance. By continuing to achieve the successes celebrated during Black History Month, blacks continue to combat racism.

In light of the contemporary absence of significant institutional barriers, black progress is largely independent of the retrograde attitudes of a few white racists. The out-dated approaches of the 1960s keep many blacks from seeing this new reality. A more realistic and hopeful America seeks more ways to empower blacks and other minorities spiritually, socially, politically, and economically. This empowerment comes not from government favors or ethno-centrism but from the God-given realization of one's own inherent dignity that flourishes in freedom and the rule of law.

DEVALUING THE BLACK FAMILY

Forty-three percent of black pregnancies end in abortion, according to a recent study by the Alan Guttmacher Institute, a leading research and advocacy organization promoting sex education. Nearly 70 percent of all black children are born out-of-wedlock. These two facts taken together clearly demonstrate the marriage and family crisis in black America. During the upcoming presidential campaign, the candidates will likely focus on affirmative action and racial injustice, but no one will mention the black American marriage and family crisis.

For demagogues, such unbalanced racial statistics necessarily imply discrimination. Employing this popular political logic, the numbers suggest that abortion providers are racist and that states racially discriminate when issuing marriage licenses. The explanation lies elsewhere.

Americans must question the country's general moral climate when black women choose to abort nearly half of their pregnancies. What motivates this preference for abortion and disdain for marriage? Data on family life necessarily raises important questions about the moral choices people make. What's more, one should ask searching questions of the churches—are they teaching their congregations the dignity and value of human life, marriage, family, and community?

Interestingly, the severity of social problems within black communities has intensified since the civil rights victories of the 1960s. In 1960, when black America seemed to be relatively worse off, only 23 percent of black kids were born out-of-wedlock. In 1970, just 33 percent of black women aged 20–29 were unmarried. By 1992, the number of unmarried twenty-something black women catapulted to 70 percent. A gross misconception about the out-of-wedlock birth crisis in black communities is that it results from teenage pregnancy. In fact, out-of-wedlock birth rates are the highest among women between the ages of 18 and 29. Moreover, since 1969, black women between the ages of 20 and 24 account for the largest increase in out-of-wedlock births. It appears, therefore, that contemporary adult black women deliberately choose to bear children outside of marriage.

Living with married parents profoundly affects a black child's quality of life. A data analysis report on marriage released by the Heritage Foundation highlights several benefits of marriage. For example, marriage dramatically reduces the incidence of poverty for women who remain romantically involved with the father from the time of the child's birth. Marriage reduces the odds that a mother and child will live in poverty by more than 70 percent. If mothers remain single and unemployed, they will remain poor permanently; if single and employed at least part-time, slightly more than half will slip below the poverty line. Only 10 percent of mothers will sink into poverty if employed full-time. Moreover, marriage combined with part-time maternal employment increases family income by 75 percent. Sadly, over 80 percent of long-term child poverty occurs in broken or never-married families.

Even more alarming pathologies result from out-of-wedlock births. For example, nearly 30 percent of all welfare recipients resort to living on public assistance because of poverty associated with single-parenthood. Black children from single-parent homes are twice more likely to commit crimes than black children from families with resident fathers. Seventy percent of juveniles in state reform institutions come from single-parent homes. In addition, there is a strong, inverse relationship between the incidence of out-of-wedlock births and education attainment.

Of course, individuals can and do rise above brokenness and poverty. Yet, the statistical big picture reveals how the devaluation of marriage and family has created a crisis in many black communities. The Bush Administration proposes making marriage an important component of the next phase of welfare reform, and rightly so. The administration seeks to introduce incentives to increase and maintain a high number of marriages in an effort to thwart many of the associated outcomes listed above.

A government program, however, can only go so far. More than ever before, this country desperately needs churches to step in and proactively address this issue. America needs a strong witness from Christians who can communicate persuasively and practice God's design for marriage, family, and community. Disconnecting human life, marriage, and family from their correct foundation in God is literally destroying communities and keeping generations enslaved to self-destructive behavior.

Reverend Ray Hammond, pastor of Bethel AME Church and board member of Boston's Black Ministerial Alliance, has the right idea. Rev. Hammond promotes biblical formulations of marriage and family in hopes of combating what he calls "the epidemic level of fatherlessness in America." He understands that marriage, rightly constructed, is necessary in providing the way out of "the social wilderness of family disintegration."

Given a culture that stifles human potential through abortion and the devaluation of the bedrock, life-sustaining institution of the family, one should not be surprised by the absence of "enough" black presence in influential sectors of American society. Many people forget the time when these pathologies were the exception rather than the rule in the black community. Overcoming these problems requires rediscovering God's wisdom, including a right understanding of the institutions that strengthen families and build up communities.

PART TWO

Politics / Economics

GOVERNMENT HEALTH CARE:
BACK TO THE PLANTATION

PRINCETON RELIGION PROFESSOR CORNEL West asserts in his 2008 book, *Hope on a Tight Rope* that "the very discovery that black people are human beings is a new one." If his statement is correct, than should not blacks question centralizing health care decisions made by bureaucratic officials only recently cognizant of minorities' humanity? "White brothers and sisters have been shaped by 244 years of white supremacist slavery, 87 years of white supremacist Jim and Jane Crow, and then another 40 years in which progress has been made" but "the stereotypes still cut deep," West wrote. He admits "relative progress for a significant number of black people," but warns that there has not been "some kind of fundamental transformation" in America. Dr. West asserts that "white supremacy is married to capitalism." If this were true, then why would blacks want to set up a health-care system that strengthens the government sanction of health-care provision by businesses?

If Georgetown University sociology professor Michael Eric Dyson is correct, current Black leaders constantly remind America of its racism. Should not these same leaders protest the expansion of government control contained in the health-care reform bill currently working its way through Congress?

Here is why. Notwithstanding their rhetoric of freedom and empowerment, many prominent black leaders appear content to send blacks back to the government plantation—where a small number of Washington elites make decisions for blacks who are not in the room.

Why do minority leaders not favor alternatives that demonstrate faith in the intelligence and dignity of people to manage their own lives?

In a sermon at Howard University, the Rev. Jeremiah Wright reminded university students that, "Racism is alive and well. Racism is how this country was founded and how this country is still run." During the presidential campaign, Wright explained to his parishioners that America is "a country and culture controlled by rich white people." However, if racists and "rich white people" control America, why do Wright's sympathizers assume that those same people will look out for the health of blacks?

If Georgetown University professor Michael Dyson is correct about racial and structural injustice impeding poor blacks, then there is cause for concern. In response to Bill Cosby's "conservative" reflections on black America in 2006, the Rev. Dr. Dyson wrote, "Cosby is hell bent on denying that race and structural forces play any role in the lives of the poor." He continued by saying, "The plane of black progress lifts on the wings of personal responsibility and social justice." Unfortunately, Dr. Dyson's "plane of black progress" is taxiing in circles on the tarmac because its twin wing engines, "personal responsibility" and "social justice," sputtered out. To carry the analogy further, the plane's passengers remain strapped in their seats, waiting for someone to rescue them, and cursing the autopilot, for none of them knows how to fly the plane. Encouraging poor blacks to embrace personal responsibility and justice would shift their focus from the past to the present and future, from passive resignation to positive action. It is time to stop being a passenger and learn to fly the plane.

CNN analyst Roland Martin stated on February 18, 2009, "While everyone seems to be caught up in the delusion of a post-racial America, we cannot forget the reality of the racial America, where African-Americans were treated and portrayed as inferior and less than others." If Martin is correct, blacks ought to be concerned about centralized health care, which will tether them ever more securely to a fundamentally corrupt political system. Blacks cannot hope for change, after all: Martin insists that "the realities of race" are "being played out in our communities each day," and had noted earlier that when it comes to white racism, blacks should "accept the fact that some people will not change" (September 10, 2008).

Many black leaders seem confused on this point. If America has a race problem, then it will manifest itself in both public and private sectors. Expanding Medicare and Medicaid only subjects poor blacks to more government control. Economic empowerment and returning health decisions to black people are the only way to eradicate concerns about structural injustice. Health-care providers competing for black patronage would empower blacks and give them control over their own destinies. Economic freedom in health care is a moral and civil-rights issue because for too long blacks have suffered the indignity of having political structures make surrogate decisions about their bodies.

Black leaders should encourage policymakers to make health-care more affordable by giving individuals absolute control over their earnings with concomitant power to choose their own healthcare plan. Instead, they are conspiring with Congress to lead poor blacks back to the plantation.

TOO MUCH GOVERNMENT MAKES US SICK

While Congress is busy working on health care reform, policy-makers are reluctant to admit that many of our nation's health problems result from practices subsidized by taxpayers. An American diet heavily dependent on corn and corn-derivatives is linked to obesity, coronary heart disease, high blood pressure, Type II-Diabetes, constipation, joint pain, and other ailments. The tragic irony is that government subsidizes the low-cost production of the corn-based, unhealthy foods that make many people sick. Now the Obama administration wants to give these same policy-makers responsibility for our health care.

According to the Environmental Workers Group, corn subsidies in the United States totaled $56.2 billion from 1995–2006. This government intervention has encouraged the widespread use of corn syrup as a sweetener in many manufactured foods. Yet, many of the unhealthiest foods are those with the highest levels of high-fructose corn syrup. In effect, government subsidies have made unhealthy foods extremely cheap to produce. An unbelievable number of products now contain significant amounts of corn syrup, ranging from salad dressing to hot dogs.

Government policy-makers regularly prove themselves unwise decision-makers by continuing to introduce arbitrary agricultural price distortions, thus creating incentives for producing unhealthy food through farm subsidies. Perhaps the most effective national health care initiative moving forward would be allowing markets to function so that people can make better food choices.

Good stewardship of one's body or nature requires possessing accurate information on which to base decisions. Prices help to convey that information. For example, what would happen if the market determined actual corn prices? Not subsidizing corn would cause a needed price correction. Perhaps fast-food value-meals would adjust in price, creating disincentives for eating unhealthy diets. Without corn and other agricultural subsidies, perhaps the price of meat would adjust to a point encouraging different choices benefiting everyone in the end. For example, eating a 72-ounce steak at the Big Texan restaurant in Amarillo, Texas would be too expensive to consider.

While individuals are ultimately responsible to exercise good stewardship in choosing what and how much to eat, incentives suffer distortion by government meddling in the market. Dr. Barry Sears, author of *Toxic Fat: When Good Fat Turns Bad*, argues, "The problem lies with America's continually subsidizing of corn and soybean production." Government subsidies generate "an oversupply of cheap refined carbohydrates and cheap vegetable oils that when combined give rise to increased diet-induced inflammation." This inflammation in turn "activates the genes in people who are genetically predisposed to gain weight with relative ease," giving rise to all the health problems connected to excessive weight. Estimates for medical spending on obesity reached $147 billion in 2008, an 87 percent increase in the past decade.

The August 31, 2009 issue of *Time Magazine* similarly noticed the corn subsidy link to America's diet and health-care problems. The story explains why, in most fast-food restaurants, a burger, fries, and soft-drink costs about $5—"a bargain, given that the meal contains nearly 1,200 calories, more than half the daily recommended requirement for adults," writes Bryan Walsh. Notably, the $100-billion fast food industry and the $23 billion snack food industry rely on corn subsidized by taxpayers. Is it any wonder that junk food tends to saturate lower-income neighborhoods?

Thanks in part to government policy-makers, unhealthy food is cheap and the cost of treating diet-related medical problems is exploding. A consensus concludes that a healthier American diet would lead to better overall health and reduced healthcare costs.

The bottom line is this: to achieve a healthier America, the government should no longer subsidize farmers one penny, resulting in a free market that would provide the information needed to make good decisions. The Obama administration and Congress would do the country an enormous favor if they stopped asking Americans to assist producing food that contributes to poor nutrition and poor health. This would be real progress toward better stewardship of the human body and the earth.

A RACIST RECESSION?

Looking at the latest unemployment numbers, conspiracy theorists might postulate that the current economic crisis shows a racial dimension, a tilting against blacks and especially black males. The latest seasonally adjusted U.S Bureau of Labor Statistics unemployment numbers reveal that blacks have an unemployment rate of 13.3 percent compared to 7.9 percent for whites. For black men over nineteen years of age, the data are even worse: 15.4 percent compared to 8 percent for white males. These gaps represent a terrible cost in lost potential, and require action on multiple fronts. Critical changes to resolve this problem include reforming welfare policies in tandem with renewing an ethic of educational achievement.

High black unemployment has more to do with lags in educational attainment and skill acquisition than with racism. In tight economic seasons, employers are less able to absorb the cost of less productive labor as demand for products and services decreases. Employers consequently often lay off low-skilled laborers first, who then experience difficulty finding new employment. Having few skills disproportionately affects African-American males in an American economy characterized by increasing specialization and widespread illegal immigration.

To make matters worse, black males approach a high school dropout rate of 50 percent. Lacking basic education and needed skills in a down turned economy increases the chance of unemployment. Currently, those with no high school diplomas experience a 12.6 percent unemployment rate. Those with a high school diploma or college degree see rates at 8.3 percent and 4.1 percent, respectively.

These discouraging statistics have human faces. Twenty-one year-old Jimmie Jackson's experience illustrates the struggles many black men without employable skills currently confront. Although Jackson earned a high school diploma, he has not worked in three years and possesses no real job experience other working in retail and fast food industries as a teenager. To make matters worse, Jackson lives in Michigan, which suffers from the highest seasonally adjusted unemployment rate in America at 12.6 percent.

Jackson says that the hardest part of his failed three-year job search is "not getting a call back." He notes that, as a black man, he is at an additional disadvantage because of stigmas and stereotypes. "Black men have a bad rep," Jackson says about living in Grand Rapids, Michigan. Yet Jackson says he regrets playing into the stereotypes himself, conceding that he is not surprised when employers shy away from a candidate who is "all tatted up." "If I was white," he says, "I'd be afraid to hire some black dude with tattoos all over his body too." Additionally frustrating for Jackson is the wish to change his appearance and presentation but the lack of money to do so. "You can't just go buy a suit if you don't have any money."

The bleak stories behind the unemployment numbers teach a hard lesson, the consequences of remaining in low-skilled jobs too long, the importance of graduating from high school, and the importance of continuing higher education. Pursuing a good education increases the likelihood of contributing to the common good. Encouraging educational success depends in large measure on cultivating the virtue of self-betterment, an aim frustrated by government welfare.

Sadly, because of America's exploding government program menu, the virtue of "getting an education" seems irrelevant to low-income blacks. Before President Lyndon Johnson's war on poverty programs, African American parents, grandparents, pastors, teachers, and coaches emphasized to their charges—regardless of their social class—the importance of "getting an education." Black communities historically stressed the importance of learning and training as prerequisites for living better than the previous generation,

Before government promised to meet one's every need, and because of previous experiences with the oppressive potential of government, black children regularly heard from their elders that the key to living beyond subsistence meant acquiring as much education as possible. A good education creates opportunities and options. It is no accident that the civil-rights movement gathered steam with Brown v. Board of Education of Topeka, Kansas, the unanimous decision ruling that segregation in public schools was unconstitutional.

For young men like Jackson living on "public assistance," the promises of government programs undermine any incentive for self-improvement. Jackson says that many of his friends have simply resigned themselves to nihilism: a steady life of drug use, run-ins with the police, and living on a government check. This incentive system weakens and threatens to destroy the culture of achievement that blacks successfully built in times past.

To move forward, low-income black communities must escape the prisons of government programs, recover a sense of personal dignity, and recapture the educational mores that have served as catalyst for fulfilling and productive lives.

THE ABRACADABRA STIMULUS PLAN

The $787 billion economic stimulus President Obama signed into law this week rightly recognizes that spending stimulates the economy. That measure, however, misses the mark: targeted, demand-driven consumer spending is the engine that powers economies, not frivolous government spending for future "needs." It pays to remember what Harvard economist and past president of the American Economic Association, Frank Taussig, flatly stated in his 1911 book, *Principles of Economics*, that "We must accept the consumer as the final judge."

As recent history teaches, economic crises arouse an emotional panic, tempting Americans to believe that Federal financial planning is the spoon-fed medicine to cure an ailing economy and the best safeguard against future relapse. To make matters worse, spin-doctors lead anxiety-ridden people to swallow the placebo that, lacking government oversight, Americans are doomed. This history illustrates a serious moral temptation of economic crises: a prideful belief in man's ability to "save" the economy by controlling the decisions of the millions of human beings who participate in it every day.

The panic of the Great Depression provided incentive for the founding of the Cowles Commission for Research in Economics in 1932 by businessman and economist, Alfred Cowles. The Cowles Commission attempted to link economic theory to mathematics and statistics. Henceforth, many economists operated on the misguided presumption that they could predict the future preferences of consumers by using math. This wizardly attempt to pair mathematical equations to the future desires of 300 million people exhibits the same kind of hubris that underlies the idea of spending billions of dollars to create artificial demand for so-called "new jobs."

On April 19, 1933, in one of the initial attempts by government to manage the economy, the United States went off the gold standard by a presidential proclamation. Franklin Roosevelt nationalized gold owned by private citizens and abrogated contracts in which payment was specified in gold. Nearly 445,000 newly minted gold $20 "Double Eagle" coins were destroyed. On June 5, 1933, Congress voided all gold clauses in public and private debts.

In 1936, John Maynard Keynes published *The General Theory of Employment, Interest* and *Money*, suggesting that the classic model that Taussig supported was a special case and applied only in times of full employment. At volatile and anxious times, Keynes asserted, the economy needed an activist government to create full employment. Tinkering by sage public officials would be more successful than the free operation of economic actors, human persons. Keynes advised governments to increase money supply to overcome depression, a recommendation that influenced the New Deal and one that echoes in Obama's recovery plan.

On November 11, 1940, Frank Taussig died, and with him died the common sense theory that the consumer is the final arbiter of economic growth. If consumers trade cash for desired goods and services, consumers control economic growth. Obama's plan to create 3.5 million jobs, many of which will come from transportation, environmental, broadband, and other infrastructure projects, seems to misunderstand this key principle. For example, why do "green jobs" not exist? Perhaps these jobs do not exist because Americans do not want "green" products. Is it wise, then, to invent preferences that people do not have? Creating jobs that are not in demand and making expensive products that people do not want or need will not stimulate the economy in the long run. Simple pride attempts to rework the character of the economy into an image that fits better one's own ideological proclivities.

House Speaker Nancy Pelosi (D-CA) said the stimulus bill is a deposit on the nation's progress. "By investing in new jobs, in science and innovation, in energy, in education . . .we are investing in the American people, which is the best guarantee of the success of our nation," she said. Does throwing borrowed cash at unproven programs really translate into "investing?" Is this experiment not overly burdensome to future generations who will be left holding the bag?

Whatever legislative incantation lawmakers use to attempt to change future consumer spending preferences, as long as consumers feel insecure about their futures the economy will remain sluggish. Real need generates real demand, which, in turn, creates sustainable jobs. Arrogance leads politicians to believe they can fix the economy by waving the wand of government spending. However, magic economic spells do not work and will only create the conditions, a generation hence, for the perceived need of another government stimulus package.

PROTECTING THE POOR FROM THE MEDIA'S GAS TAX

Why do so-called progressives seem eager to ignore the real needs of the poor? A recent example was the New York Times editorial calling on President-Elect Obama to institute a random gasoline tax to keep gas prices from dropping below $4 per gallon (in 2008 dollars) to "curb the nation's demand for energy." The proposal is fraught with problems, among which would be its impact on those who can least afford the burdensome tax.

In "The Gas Tax," the *Times* editors say, "it might be time for the president-elect and Congress to think seriously about imposing a gas tax or similar levy to keep gas prices up after the economy recovers from recession."

This lunacy fits a pattern. In a December 7 interview with President-Elect Barack Obama, on NBC's *Meet the Press*, Tom Brokaw suggested, in light of dropping fuel prices, that government should "take this opportunity to put a tax on gasoline, bump it back up to $4 a gallon where people were prepared to pay for that, and use that revenue for alternative energy and as a signal to the consumers those days are gone."

Why do the most prominent media voices seem so ignorant of the economic consequences of their social experiments?

Obama responded, "Well, keep, keep in mind what's happening in—to families all across America. Yes, gas prices have gone down. However, in the meantime, maybe somebody in the family's lost their job. In the meantime, their housing values have plummeted. In the meantime, maybe their hours have been cut back. Or if they're a small-business owner, their sales have gone down 50, 60, 70 percent. So putting additional burdens on American families right now, I think, is a mistake."

Obama demonstrated better economic common sense than did the journalists on this point. Why needlessly hurt lower-income Americans with a "consumption tax" disproportionately making life worse for rural and inner city residents, ethnic minorities, single-mothers, and other struggling Americans? While those who enjoy high salaries like Tom Brokaw, the editors of the *New York Times*, and other like-minded social experimenters may not feel the pinch, "bumping up" gas prices in a recession seems simply immoral.

The editors of the *Times* might gain some insight by reading their own newspaper. On June 9, 2008, the *Times* published, "Rural U.S. Takes Worst Hit as Gas Tops $4 Average," reporting the painful reality of rural Americans suffering because of high gas prices.

The article tells the story of Anthony Clark, a farm worker from Tchula, Mississippi who said he prayed "every night for lower gasoline prices. He recently decided not to fix his broken 1992 Chevrolet Astro van because he could not afford the fuel. Now he hires friends and family members to drive him around to buy food and medicine for his diabetic aunt, and his boss sends a van to pick him up for the 10-mile commute to work."

"As gas prices rise, working less could be the economically rational choice," said Tim Slack, a sociologist at Louisiana State University who studies rural poverty. "That would mean lower incomes for the poor and greater distance from the mainstream."

In a June 29, 2008 *New York Times* editorial, "Fuel for Inequality," Robert Reich, former secretary of labor and professor of public policy at the University of California, Berkeley, explains why high fuel prices increase the wage gap between the haves and have-nots. Rural residents "tend to drive older cars that get lousy mileage. They don't trade them in as often as wealthier people do, and can't afford hybrids or new models that use gas more efficiently. And it's not unusual for their jobs to require them to haul stuff from one place to another in pickup trucks or vans that guzzle even more gas."

The original intent of the December 27 editorial was to propose a way to encourage Americans to purchase the fuel-efficient cars U.S. automakers promised as they received bailout cash from taxpayers, but the consequences hurt all Americans in the end.

A mistaken gas consumption tax will not force Americans to buy automobiles we do not want from Detroit automakers who cannot compete with international companies technologically ahead of them. Although the *New York Times* urges Detroit to produce more fuel-efficient cars, the automakers need the impetus to make affordable vehicles that perform better than their European and Asian competitors do. Design and performance innovation, unlike tax-inflated gas prices, might actually benefit working class Americans, the very people progressives allegedly support and champion

UNEMPLOYMENT AND SOCIAL COHESION

As the U.S. economy continues to slide into a recession, truly disadvantaged Americans, those less able to absorb the economic shock, must remain a priority. With deep job cuts in retail, manufacturing, and construction contributing to the highest unemployment rate in fourteen years, American society must confront the implications of the minimum wage in those sectors and the effects of joblessness in low-come neighborhoods.

The current unemployment numbers are more alarming because of the relationship between employment and social cohesion. High unemployment levels profoundly affect the social stability of American families and communities. A dynamic relationship exists between economic life and moral life. High levels of joblessness are catalysts for breakdowns in social organization with issues ranging from crime, violence, and drug trafficking to break downs in marriage and family life.

Also affected are intermediate institutions that make communities work. Working families are in a better position to support churches, community and non-profit organizations, recreational facilities, and the like. When these institutions decline, the many ways in which these intermediate institutions foster civil society also decline sharply.

According to the Labor Department, in 2008 unemployment rate rose to 6.5 percent, with an increase in the number of unemployed persons by 603,000 to 10.1 million. Over the past 12 months, the number of unemployed persons has increased by 2.8 million, and the unemployment rate has risen by 1.7 percentage points. The unemployment rates rose for adult men (6.3 percent), adult women (5.3 percent), whites (5.9 percent), and Hispanics (8.8 percent). The jobless rates for teenagers (20.6 percent) and blacks (11.1 percent) remained stable, while the unemployment rate for Asians was 3.8 percent. Recent increases in the minimum wage have compounded economic problems.

In his book, *Basic Economics*, Thomas Sowell posits that a surplus of capable workers creates unemployment more often in economies with minimum wage laws than in those with truly free markets. If American employers had the freedom to pay less, rather than laying off employees, one can imagine the resulting drop in unemployment.

It is no coincidence that many lower-skilled labor sectors experience de facto job losses. The Labor Department reports that total nonfarm payroll employment fell by 240,000 in October, bringing job losses thus far in 2008 to 1.2 million. Employment declines are heavily leveraged in manufacturing, construction, and several service-providing industries.

When revenues decline, companies cannot afford to pay workers wages that are artificially set above their productivity and demand for their skills. Additionally, laying off capable workers is not preferable in the long run because unemployed workers are not continuing to develop the skills and experience that enable them to increase their productivity or move beyond low skilled and entry-level jobs to those of higher pay.

Only economic history can provide the definitive narrative regarding the additional role the recent increase in the minimum wage is playing in the current surge in joblessness. Back in 2007, Congress voted to increase the minimum wage to $6.55 per hour effective July 24, 2008 and $7.25 per hour effective July 24, 2009.

The U.S. Chamber of Commerce opposed a minimum wage increase because it destroys entry-level jobs, stunts new job growth, and harms small businesses. In a 2007 survey, the Chamber found that 60 percent of small business owners would not be able to offset the cost of the minimum wage increase. That, in turn, would lead businesses to make tough decisions like slashing benefits, raising prices, and laying off workers.

Although many industrialized countries have minimum wage laws, there are many exceptions, including Norway, Sweden, Finland, Denmark, Switzerland, Germany, Austria, Italy, and Cyprus. Switzerland has no minimum-wage laws and one of the lowest unemployment rates in the world. The latest numbers are 2.6 percent.

In manufacturing, construction, and retail sectors, for example, one can only wonder how many jobs would remain available if labors unions and government did not force companies to set wages higher than what the job is worth.

The way out of this recession should include establishing the conditions for companies to negotiate wages freely with current and potential employees. The most essential need from unemployed workers is a job. Any income in a tight market is better than no income. Workers who continue to work and therefore improve their job skills are better off than those capable workers who sit idle.

If economic history were any tutor, President-Elect Obama and Congress would do well to free the private sector from the regulatory shackles that stifle job creation. But if the new administration is simply going to do the bidding of Big Labor, the prospect of regulatory reform seems remote. A good place to start, however, would be taking a cue from countries like Switzerland. The results speak for themselves.

MOVING ON, WITHOUT WRIGHT

Watching Jeremiah Wright's variety show the past few weeks has been nothing less than painful. With last week's North Carolina and Indiana primary results, however, the spectacle is now moot. Wright's antics may have bruised Barack Obama's credibility, but he remains the likely Democratic presidential candidate. It is time to banish Wright and his bad theology back to obscurity.

America can safely lay Jeremiah Wright to rest because he is not the pope of the black church; he speaks only for himself. According to a Selig Center study, approximately 46,000 predominantly African American Christian congregations exist in this country. Nearly 86 percent of African American Christians belong to historically black denominations. Jeremiah Wright represents one voice from one congregation. Wright's black liberation theology and "the black church" are not synonymous.

If Jerry Falwell does not represent all white Protestants, then it follows that there is no reason to accept Wright's assertion that to attack him is to attack the black church. Jeremiah Wright has severely damaged the image of the black church, as many will now wrongly associate his extreme separatist views with the black church in general

Wright is merely a footnote in history because he is not and never has been Obama's mentor or spiritual advisor. Wright's confession of his own self-promotion, when he suggested that Obama's distancing was merely political, tells the true story. If Wright really cared about Obama and was close to him, Wright would have kept his mouth closed until after the Democratic convention. Real friends do whatever it takes to promote the other's success. Wright, however, took the self-aggrandizing bait, appeared on Bill Moyers Journal, and spoke at the National Press Club.

Most painful about Obama's latest announcement of his official relational divorce from Wright was the realization of Wright's betrayal. Obama's inability to rein in his former friend, during the most important event in Obama's political life, displayed Wright's willingness to let Obama endure painful backlash. Obama, possibly unfamiliar with the kind of person Wright really is, should have used stronger language to distance himself earlier from his former pastor.

Finally, Wright is irrelevant because he is not running for president. America has critical issues to discuss other than the possibility of Wright's residual effect on Obama's ideology. In all honesty, most Americans do not follow what their pastors teach either. One has only to look at the profound lack of moral virtue overwhelming American culture for evidence.

Barack Obama is a "New Deal," "War on Poverty," Democrat preaching "change" to a young generation who seem economically naive and historically ignorant, willing to repeat a history of failed programs that tethered generations to intravenous government welfare and intervention. For example, though the minimum wage hurts poor people in the long-run, Obama's website says he plans to significantly "raise the minimum wage and index it to inflation to make sure that full-time workers can earn a living wage that allows them to raise their families and pay for basic needs such as food, transportation, and housing."

Obama also promises that he "will establish a federal investment program to help manufacturing centers modernize and Americans learn the new skills they need to produce green products." A "federal investment program"? Has government proven to be a skilled investor of taxpayers' money? The American government is already running a $9 trillion deficit: why would Americans trust unaccountable officials with "investing" in anything?

For those who are concerned about the poor being liberated from the shackles of dependence, the minimal standards of wealth creation and real opportunities for the poor, the possibility of at least two Supreme Court retirements during the next presidential term, and the increasingly unchecked power of government regulatory agencies, the chief concern is not whether Obama has been influenced by the spurious worldview of a former friend. It is whether he has embraced the demonstrably futile policies of FDR and LBJ.

SOWELL'S FACTS ANNIHILATE POLITICAL FICTIONS

"Truth is stranger than fiction," Mark Twain said. In politics, truth is usually irrelevant and fictional fallacies turn into public policy. Thomas Sowell has spent his entire career teaching the difference between political rhetoric and economic facts. His latest book, *Economic Facts and Fallacies*, is his most lucid missile against fictions Americans easily believe about a wide range of subjects: urban life, gender issues, education, income trends, race, and globalization.

Sowell begins by pointing out that fallacies, though fictional, have real-world consequences because their plausibility arouses political support. Among the most prominent is the myth "that economic transactions are a zero-sum process, in which what is gained by someone is lost by someone else." The idea that Americans acquire wealth by exploiting the poor illustrates this fallacy very clearly

Zero-sum politics opens the public policy door to other sorts of fallacies including the idea that focusing on the needs of one particular group has no effect on others—as if robbing Peter to pay Paul creates net benefits to society. Or that third-party surrogates must manage the details of free people's private lives and society as a whole. Or that resources are not limited and do not have alternative uses.

A decades-old urban fallacy is that government housing increases housing opportunities for the poor but, in fact, government housing annihilates new development and incentives for maintenance, thereby increasing housing shortages.

Fallacies about gender differences in employment, pay, and promotion loom large while the factual data tell a different story. Policymakers tend to ignore the fact that women have to make different tradeoffs than do men. Women's decisions about motherhood profoundly affect lifetime earnings, work tenure, and choice of employment.

In fact, never-married women with no children earn just as much as men within their peer group. For example, never-married women from forty to sixty-three-years-old, the peak wage-earning years, collect average salaries that are $7,000 per year higher than men.

In education, Sowell states that college costs rise because educational institutions have few constraints on their spending. The federal government, using taxpayers' money, subsidizes frivolous and arbitrary spending choices at the hands of administrators, professors, and athletics departments.

Racial comparisons between blacks and whites afford very little information about so-called institutional discrimination. Discussions on race usually omit data on Asian Americans, which would challenge many Americans' assumptions. For example, Asians are likelier than whites to receive bank loans, and on average, higher academic grades and test scores. Does that mean that the ACT discriminates against whites and favors Asians?

One of the most pathetic myths about globalization is a rehashing of Lenin's idea that industrialized countries maintain their wealth by exploiting poor countries. Again, reality tells a different story. Countries that remain among the poorest in the world are those with the least foreign capital investment. Developing countries are poor and remain poor for a myriad of reasons that do not involve the revisionist causal claims of "imperialism." Moreover, since conquest, war, slavery, migration, poverty, and geographic challenges trouble the histories of all nations, the pertinent question is, what allows some nations to create wealth while others fail? Those nations that prosper and enjoy the most freedom also value basic morality, property rights, and the rule of law.

There is a deeper lesson here. Many of the fallacies Sowell dissects rely on the tendency to treat people as faceless parts of an aggregate rather than as unique individuals possessing inherent dignity. Popular but misguided policies designed to combat poverty, discrimination, and underdevelopment gained public approval because humanity lost sight of the true nature of human beings, human behavior, and man's created destiny. Sowell's book is a wonderful exhortation to return to common sense by distinguishing truth from fiction.

IT'S ABOUT OBAMA'S ECONOMICS, NOT HIS FAITH

Attempts to align Barack Obama with the views of his recently retired pastor, Rev. Jeremiah Wright, distract Americans from Obama's actual platform. Obama's membership in Chicago's Trinity United Church of Christ may not reveal much about what Obama believes personally. Charges of guilt-by-association miss the mark and expose general ignorance about Protestant liberalism and mainline black churches. Concerned voters should instead focus on Obama's economic policies, which are troubling enough.

In a recent statement, Obama's campaign said he "does not think of the pastor of his church in political terms. Like a member of his family, there are things he says with which Senator Obama deeply disagrees." In the context of black church life, this makes complete sense. Unlike white evangelical churches, many black congregations do not typically tie personal religious convictions to public policy prescriptions. This explains the phenomenon that puzzles some observers: Many blacks can be culturally conservative and yet vote with liberal democrats

Jeremiah Wright's embrace of black liberation theology and Afrocentrism does not necessarily mean that Barack Obama does. The only part of Obama's campaign rhetoric that sounds remotely like black liberation theology is his belief that government will solve all of America's problems by redistributing wealth from the upper classes to the proletariat and erecting government as a surrogate decision-maker for the masses. It is possible that Obama does not take the faith principles he learned under Wright as seriously as he claims.

Instead of straining a gnat through a straw to make a connection between Obama's beliefs and those of Wright, the pertinent question remains: What initiatives does Obama plan to spearhead in the Republic? Obama is not running a campaign that is "unashamedly Black and unapologetically Christian," as Trinity UCC's website professes. Afrocentrism does not win primaries but promising government as the cure-all does.

In fact, what is far more worrisome than Trinity's "commitment to Africa" or her commitment to the "historical education of African people in Diaspora" is the call for "economic parity." Economic parity, or more notably economic equality, is the justification for an exploding welfare and entitlement state. The race critique of black liberation theology serves as a distraction from a true socialist agenda.

Economic parity implies government-coerced wealth redistribution, perpetual minimum wage increases, government subsidized health care for all, and so on. One of the priorities listed on his campaign website reads, "Obama will protect tax cuts for poor and middle class families, but he will reverse most of the Bush tax cuts for the wealthiest taxpayers." Does this sound familiar? Obama supports socialized medicine: "Obama will make available a new national health plan to all Americans, including the self-employed and small businesses, to buy affordable health coverage that is similar to the plan available to members of Congress." A "national health plan"? The former Soviet Union attempted this, as well.

It gets worse. Obama wants to create socialized wages: "Obama will raise the minimum wage and index it to inflation to make sure that full-time workers can earn a living wage that allows them to raise their families and pay for basic needs such as food, transportation, and housing." All of these government-controlled, state-run, taxpayer funded initiatives are all efforts to move disadvantaged blacks toward greater parity.

If Obama's church focuses on blacks in the Chicago area and African people here and abroad, who cares? Good for them. Is anyone paying attention to what Obama wants to use government to achieve? CNBC economic analyst Larry Kudlow estimates that Obama's vision for government-run everything is going to cost Americans $800 billion. That money will come from taxing the rich, the middle-class, household pets, and anything else that has life.

Make utopian promises, tax, spend, redistribute. There is nothing new under the sun, Ecclesiastes says. For all of Obama's apparent appeal as fresh and new, Americans are dealing here with the familiar and conventional religious left: lots of Jesus-talk supporting an economic platform that attempts to resurrect Karl Marx. If Obama is selected as the Democrats' candidate, his connection to Wright will be the least of our 800 billion worries.

'WAR ON POVERTY' REMIX WON'T WORK EITHER

"There is nothing new under the sun." The oft-quoted saying from the book of Ecclesiastes is especially true of John Edwards' well-intentioned but misguided "poverty tour." Edwards' proposals to help the poor are nothing more than a remix of Franklin Roosevelt's "New Deal" and Lyndon Johnson's "War on Poverty" and, like those previous initiatives, miss the mark.

Government wealth redistribution, larger labor unions, and expanded government social programs failed the poor in the past and will continue to fail the truly disadvantaged in the future.

Raising the minimum wage fails to help the poor over the long term. It is emotionally comforting to assume that arbitrary wage inflations will give the poor more cash but, in fact, the economics do not work that way.

James Sherk of the Heritage Foundation reiterates three important truths. First, the only workers who benefit from a higher minimum wage are those who actually earn that higher wage. A higher minimum wage causes employers to cut back on both the number of workers they hire and their employees' working hours, which reduces overall job opportunities for the poor.

Second, few minimum wage earners actually come from poor households. The beneficiaries of higher minimum wages are unlikely to be poor because most minimum-wage earners are not poor—they tend instead to be groups such as suburban teens. Third, the poorest of Americans do not work at all, for any wage, so raising the minimum wage does not help them. The raise actually guarantees that the truly disadvantaged remain unemployable. Sherk reports that each 10 percent increase in the minimum wage reduces employment in affected groups of workers by roughly 2 percent. Thus, raising the minimum wage to $7.25 an hour could cause at least 8 percent of affected workers to lose their jobs in the end. Real wages rise when there is a proliferation of free enterprise creating greater competition between employers for low skilled labor.

Labor unions do not help the truly disadvantaged either. America's labor unions exist to promote their own protectionist interests instead of the interests of the unskilled, common man. Labor unions love minimum wage increases because they make unskilled labor too expensive for employers. As a result, says Sherk, skilled labor becomes more attractive, potentially raising the earnings of union members by 20 to 40 percent as they compete with minimum wage workers for jobs. In the end, non-union, low-skilled workers' earnings actually fall due to reduced working hours and fewer job opportunities. This explains why many minimum wage workers rarely have jobs allowing 40 hours per week and why companies abandon low-income neighborhoods.

WHAT KIND OF LONG-TERM HELP IS THAT?

Finally, government cannot create one of the most critical ingredients in long-term poverty amelioration: responsible fathers. Responsible fathering is a moral issue. On what ground do politicians and government bureaucrats speak about responsible fathering? It is not mentioned in the Constitution. Is America left to glean principles from politicians' behavior and private conduct? In recent decades, presidents betrayed their wives by dating actresses and committing sexual acts with college interns. Additionally, many Congressmen engage in adulterous sex with staffers or hire prostitutes from D.C. streets and high-end "escort" services.

Responsible fathering results not from receiving cash assistance but from building a morally formed sense of integrity, responsibility, and character. No government program can develop a man's identity nor cultivate a disposition of life-long committed love, affection, and duty to his wife and children. However, government can support fatherhood by ensuring conditions for the free operation of the intermediate institutions—families, churches, fraternal societies—that have historically and successfully formed men.

Government, on the other hand, can interfere with marriage and provide disincentives for fatherly responsibility, as demonstrated during America's experiment with pre-1996 welfare programs that subsidized, and therefore encouraged, fatherlessness.

While poverty tours heighten public awareness of the problem, remixing failed ideologies does nothing more than guarantee future "poverty tours" among the same unaffected poor populations.

LET THE AIRLINE MERGERS BEGIN

As U.S. Airways proceeds with its hostile $8 billion bid for bankrupt Delta Airlines Inc., some worry that the move will mean fewer options, less competition, and higher prices. The more probable result is the contrary. A more extensive consolidation of the airline industry should be welcomed. If not thwarted by the government and labor unions, consolidation will make the 130 carriers now flying more efficient and competitive, delivering multiple benefits, including more options and lower prices, to consumers.

Consolidation would be compatible with the practice of stewardship, which views the goods of this world—including business enterprises—as being held in trust and thereby entailing an obligation on their trustees to manage their concerns in a manner that is not wasteful or destructive. Given the nature of the industry today, proper stewardship of commercial airlines implies reform.

Without taxpayer protection, Delta Air Lines would be no more. In October, Delta reported that its net loss narrowed to $88 million from $301 million in the same month of last year. Delta is in serious trouble and a U.S. Airways consolidation would bring increased pressure to instate a sustainable business operation.

Under the protection of the government's lenient bankruptcy laws and maladroit interference with the free market, major airlines such as Delta have been able to survive the market driven fates of Eastern, Pan Am, and Trans World Airlines.

The airline industry has perfected the art of seeking government protection in bankruptcy to disguise their own mismanagement and to shield themselves from unions seeking to leverage arbitrary wage inflation that companies cannot afford. Flying under bankruptcy actually provides an unfair advantage over competitors. Bankrupt airlines continue to lose money without facing market consequences. Bankruptcy protection, therefore, retards growth in the industry and reduces competition in the end.

Consolidation of mismanaged airlines makes the industry more efficient, better able to meet consumer demand, and—contrary to popular impression—increases competition. Burdened by excess flying capacity, the top five airlines need to streamline their operations. If the top airlines were to consolidate, it would give other airlines opportunities to enter into new markets, providing consumers with more flying options. More flying options mean more competition and lower prices.

A U.S. Airways/Delta merger, considering their overlapping markets, would not leave consumers in the southeast with only one major airline, as many are foolishly projecting. On the contrary, dozens of gates would open up, giving new airlines a shot at meeting the needs of consumers.

In fact, the possibility of gate vacancies is already stirring interest. Bloomberg News, citing remarks by Chief Executive Officer Gary Kelly, reports that Southwest Airlines Co., the biggest low-fare carrier in the country, would consider buying gates, planes, and other assets sold in a US Airways/Delta Air merger. Landing slots at New York's LaGuardia airport might be among the targets.

"We would be very interested in any assets that are divested," Kelly said in an interview. The East Coast "is our least-developed region and where we are trying to grow and have had a lot of difficulty gaining access to markets."

The *Wall Street Journal* reported that AirTran Inc. Chairman and Chief Executive Joe Leonard said he is also interested in acquiring airport gates opened by a US Airways/Delta merger. Leonard said discount carrier AirTran would consider buying abandoned shuttle operations as a way to gain access to gates at New York's LaGuardia International Airport and Washington's Reagan National Airport.

If the Delta merger fails, there is speculation that United Airlines might approach Delta with an offer of its own. Either Continental or American Airlines, in the industry realignment, might then court Northwest Airlines.

All of this merger talk is a promising sign. Consumers and share-holders who desire good old-fashioned stewardship—greater efficiency, more options, and lower prices—would welcome the news of consolidations. The market is working as it should.

WELFARE REFORM IS WORKING

August 22, 2006 marked the tenth anniversary of welfare reform. The 1996 legislation made radical changes to the process of receiving un-earned government cash. The results have been massive reductions in child poverty, increases in employment, and a subsequent increase in the freedom of the poor from government control.

In the mid-1990s, many politicians tried to kill the reforms by incit-ing fear. Senator Daniel Patrick Moynihan (D-NY) proclaimed the 1996 law to be "the most brutal act of social policy since Reconstruction." He ridiculously predicted, "Those involved will take this disgrace to their graves." Marian Wright Edelman, president of the Children's Defense Fund, declared the new reform law an "outrage. . . that will hurt and impoverish millions of American children." As expected, these projec-tions were dead wrong.

Robert Rector, Senior Research Fellow at the Heritage Foundation, using government data, summarized welfare reform's success before Congress.

The facts tell a powerful story: When America invites the poor to live with dignity within the structures of liberty, the poor usually re-spond admirably. Since the 1996 reforms child poverty has plummeted. Some 1.6 million fewer children live in poverty today than in 1995.

Poor black children have enjoyed the greatest decreases in poverty. After the early 1970s, reductions in black child poverty had stagnated. Since 1995, however, the poverty rate among black children has fallen at an unprecedented rate—from 41.5 percent to 32.9 percent in 2004. By 2001, black child poverty had fallen to 30 percent, the lowest point in American history. Over a six-year period after welfare reform, 1.2 million black children escaped poverty. Although recent economic corrections have slightly increased black child poverty, the rate remains about one-fifth lower than in the period prior to reform.

Unprecedented declines in poverty also occurred among children of single mothers. After 1996, the poverty rate for children of single mothers fell dramatically from 50.3 percent in 1995 to 41.9 percent in 2004. Since 1996, the employment rate of the most disadvantaged single mothers increased from 50 percent to 100 percent. Employment of single mothers who are high school dropouts rose by two-thirds, and employment of young single mothers (ages 18 to 24) nearly doubled. As mothers found employment, child poverty decreased.

Additionally, welfare caseloads dropped dramatically from 4.3 million families in 1996 to 1.89 million today. The explosive growth of out-of-wedlock births has nearly halted. As the policies of the "War on Poverty" discouraged fatherhood, the out-of-wedlock birthrate went from 7.7 percent in 1965 to 32.2 percent 1995. However since 1996 (and for several reasons besides welfare reform), the long-term rapid growth in the out-of-wedlock birth rate faltered.

A good economy alone did not produce these results. Remember, critics objected that the changes would hurt the poor during the good economy of the late 1990s. However, these results were inevitable when the government finally recognized that poor people are not "white trash" but rather, real people capable of independent thinking, caring for their families, making informed decisions and achieving success.

When society provides incentives encouraging work, marriage, family, and accountability—all central to human dignity—people routinely regarded as helpless rise to the occasion.

However, after a decade of good results, unfinished work remains. The wrong assumption still exists that poor people need government controlled surrogate decision making. Poor parents should enjoy the freedom to enroll their children in good schools; states must not economically enable those who refuse to work, and thus create poverty cycles; fatherhood and marriage should be encouraged structurally; and Americans must commit themselves to helping the poor of all races build wealth. The principles of entrepreneurship, homeownership, family, saving and investing, and commitment to community will not only lift families out of poverty but also empower them to enjoy lives of dignity for generations to come.

THE 'MORAL' MINIMUM WAGE INCREASE
HURTS TEENS AND MINORITIES

The only way to explain Republican bulldozing of the first minimum wage increase in a decade through the House of Representatives last week is election year political banditry—even though it was paired with a cut in estate taxes. Before the Senate debates this bill, it is important to remember that government-mandated minimum wage helps no one in the end. Parents of high school students and advocates for the poor should be outraged at the proposed increase because it discourages employers from hiring teenagers and low-skilled minorities.

The current wage proposal would increase the minimum wage from $5.15 per hour in three increments, reaching $7.25 in June 2009. It also allows the application of tips toward minimum wage increases in some states that currently prohibit the practice.

Emotionally, the issue is a winner—who can be against raising the prospects of the most poorly paid American workers? However, when analyzed through the lens of economics, the bill appears less rosy. Such an increase ultimately hurts teens and low-skilled minorities because minimum wage jobs are usually entry-level positions filled by employees with limited work experience and few job skills. When the government forces employers to pay their workers more than a job's productivity demands, employers, in order to stay in business, generally respond by hiring fewer hours of low-skilled labor. Low-skilled workers become too expensive to employ, creating a new army of permanent part-timers.

Americans support forced government wage increases on an emotional level—they fail to understand the economic basis of funding the wage increases. Where do the funds originate? Who or what actually pays for the wage increases? American consumers want the best products for the lowest cost. Therefore, businesses must avoid rolling the wage increase into their services and goods. Business owners and managers, instead, reduce their costs by laying off workers with the lowest skills, relocating the jobs (or the entire business) to another country, or skirting the law altogether by paying employees "under the table" or hiring illegal immigrants.

SUNY Plattsburgh economics professor D.W. MacKenzie cites figures from the Bureau of Labor Statistics that the unemployment rate for everyone over the age of 16 was 5.6 percent in 2005. Yet unemployment was 19.7 percent for those aged 16–17, while in the 18–19 age group, it was 15.8 percent. The unemployment rate for white teens in the 16–17 age group was 17.3 percent in 2005, while the same figures for Hispanic and black teens were 25 percent and 40.9 percent, respectively.

These numbers highlight the fact that the populations most likely to suffer from minimum-wage-caused unemployment are those already most at risk. University of Connecticut economics professor, Kenneth Couch, estimates that a one-dollar rise in the minimum wage in the current economic environment would further reduce teenage employment opportunities by at least 145,000—and possibly as many as 436,000—jobs.

The only groups who may be encouraged by the proposed increase are future illegal immigrants and third-world developing economies as American businesses will have to scramble to find ways to continue to provide better products at the lowest prices.

Those in favor of the increase believe that they stand on the moral high ground. Rev. Suzanne Meyer, president of All God's People, a multi-faith social advocacy group located in St. Louis, calls the current $5.15 rate "a moral outrage. It effectively sentences millions of workers and their families to live in abject poverty." Why is it not, instead, a moral outrage to increase teen unemployment, increase minority unemployment, and encourage the circumvention of the law by employing illegal immigrants and paying under the table?

Employees who become more productive by gaining experience and improving their education earn larger raises and salaries in the long term. A minimum wage set by agreement between employer and employee establishes the best entry point for people with few skills to gain experience and develop the abilities needed to advance. It is in keeping with both human dignity and economic reality to give employers and employees freedom to negotiate employment on terms set by themselves, not by politicians.

THE ANSWER IS (NOT) BLOWIN' IN THE WIND

Environmentalists deserve credit for helping Americans think seriously about their stewardship of nature. From Genesis onward, Scripture is laden with the message that creation is good, that its purpose is to manifest God's glory, and that human beings are its stewards. Man's role in creation makes it even more important to participate in truthful debates about properly stewarding the earth's resources. Capitalizing on current confusion over fossil fuel reserves, proponents of wind power are working hard to deceive concerned citizens with sensational propaganda.

Groups like the American Wind Energy Association (AWEA) and the Michigan Consumer Federation promote wind power as an energy alternative through misleading claims. "Unlike other fuels, the cost of wind never changes. It is free. And it has the added advantage of producing no pollution," says the Michigan Federation.

Wind power produces energy, says the AWEA, "without consuming any natural resources or emitting any pollution or greenhouse gases." Not only is wind power less expensive than other forms of energy production, according to the AWEA, it also increases the "security of the U.S. electricity supply."

So overwhelming are the advantages of wind power in the eyes of some proponents that they want the government to mandate that all utilities and businesses convert to wind.

Two recent studies by the Royal Academy of Engineering and the David Hume Institute blow some greatly needed fresh air into wind power's musty arguments. These studies highlight a few ways in which the wind environmentalists are deceiving consumers.

First, wind power is not free. International energy experts overwhelmingly agree that wind power will force consumers to pay twice as much as the most economical fossil-fuel alternative. The high collateral costs of using wind power leave this energy option floating dead in the water.

Both studies point to unreported capital costs like site preparation, acquisition, construction, and installation of hardware. Capital costs also include differences in the cost of electricity generated during peak versus off-peak periods.

When evaluating the feasibility of wind power, one must also factor in the net cost of maintaining and replacing existing infrastructure, as well as the cost of new construction to meet new electricity demands. Additional overhead includes employee salaries and benefits—ongoing and inflationary expenses not necessarily offset by the electricity actually generated.

Second, wind power is not pollution-free. The manufacture, installation, maintenance, and dismantling of wind turbines and towers necessitates using fossil fuels. Pollution results from producing the plastics, metal, cement, and fiberglass used in tower and turbine construction.

Third, the very operation of wind turbine fields harms the environment in certain ways. Their notorious effect on bird populations prompted the Sierra Club to tab wind towers "Cuisinarts of the air." In California alone, thousands of birds and bats, including endangered species, die in wind turbine fields every year—over 44,000 birds in the last 20 years, according to H.Sterling Burnett of the National Center for Policy Analysis. Since wind tower bases attract prey rodents, wind farms become virtual death traps for owls, hawks, and eagles.

Additionally, wind power reduces open space natural habitat. To produce just 1,000 megawatts of power, a wind farm requires about 300 square miles. That translates into 192, 000 thousand acres of land, land that must be used for the sole purpose of generating wind power. Compared to the mere 3.05 square miles needed for a conventional fossil fuel plant and the even smaller 2.65 miles needed for a secure nuclear facility, a wind farm seems less environmentally attractive.

To understand further the vast land expanse that wind farming requires, consider that New York City in the summer uses nearly 11,000 megawatts of energy. To produce wind generated power on this scale would necessitate using more than 2million acres of land.

The Washington, D.C. based AWEA, notes that the states of North Dakota, Texas, Kansas, South Dakota, and Montana possess the acreage necessary for wind farms. These undeveloped sites (and the impact from extensive wind farming, environmental and otherwise) seem to be conveniently distant from Washington, D.C.

Fourth, wind power does not necessarily equate to a secure energy supply. Wind power performs unreliably with critical capacity limitations. It is incapable of negotiating between energy demands. During peak demand there is no way to produce more energy. During low demand, there is no way to reduce energy production. As an unpredictable source of energy, wind power requires auxiliary backup by other energy sources ready for immediate use. It can never be a stand-alone energy source.

The book of Proverbs states that, "The wisdom of the prudent is to give thought to their ways, but the folly of fools is deception." Who is kidding whom? As a matter of policy, basing any significant stake on wind power would be sheer folly.

In an open market, consumers must freely deal with energy needs and resources stripped of special taxes and subsidies. To discover the most efficient methods of energy production and use, costs and pricing must be transparent to the consumer. This discovery is essential if Christians are to use resources in ways that respect their purpose, i.e., for the welfare of all and to the glory of God.

PRODUCTIVITY AND THE ICE MAN: UNDERSTANDING OUTSOURCING

Hysteria about job losses caused by overseas outsourcing ignores a crucial fact: Americans lose jobs primarily because people develop innovative ways to do things faster, better, and cheaper. In other words, human creativity is a double-edged sword, bringing productivity improvements and, very often, widespread job loss. The good news is that the net result is not fewer jobs, but more jobs—and ones that are more productive.

Since most job losses result from men and women cultivating Creation, one should never be surprised to hear that companies are downsizing. Neither should one dismiss the indisputable financial and emotional toll caused by mass layoffs or shuttered factories. However, to comprehend the situation fully requires a closer look at the fundamentals of economics. Did the layoff stem from a more productive technology, a smarter way to manufacture, or a shift in consumer preferences?

While the outsourcing issue generates headlines, it is not the chief cause of job losses. Of the 2.7 million jobs lost over the past three years, only 300,000 have resulted from outsourcing, according to Forrester Research Inc., a technology research firm. *Business Week* magazine reports that one percentage point of productivity growth can eliminate up to 1.3 million jobs a year.

Automation, a traditional means of boosting productivity, continues to eliminate jobs perforce. The sectors most affected by automation include construction, manufacturing, retail and wholesale trade, transportation, information, and food services. Airlines have reduced the number of ticket agents because of airport kiosks, online ticket purchases, and online check-in. Grocery store clerks are on the decline with the onset of automated checkout counters.

This is nothing new. As the United States industrialized, the life cycle of entire industries shrank. On July 6, 1858, for example, Lyman Blake patented a shoe-manufacturing machine. As these machines gained popularity, the need for hand-made shoes quickly disappeared— and so did related jobs. The horse and buggy industry took a hit in major cities when the first cable car, patented on January 17, 1871, by Andrew S. Hallidie, began service a couple years later. The buggy business slowly rolled to a halt when Henry Ford introduced the Model T in 1908 and then installed moving assembly lines in his factory shortly afterward. This development did not portend inevitable unemployment for the thousands of workers who, instead of making horse carriages, found other employment in the burgeoning industrial sector. The obsolescence of the horse and buggy spawned new industries (many carriage companies flourished as makers of vehicle bodies) and made human transportation exponentially more efficient.

The invention of Freon in 1928 and the introduction of electric refrigerators devastated the ice industry. Until this point, companies removed ice from the rivers and ponds, cut into it into blocks, and delivered it to insulated storage buildings for summer use. Ice wagons, first on steel wheels and later on rubber tires, carried ice to customers' homes. Because a 25-pound block of ice lasted only a few days, icemen kept busy making deliveries two or three times per week. New icemen would often give the reins to their experienced dray horses along the well-traveled routes. The horses knew the way and stopped automatically at each drop-off point. When the GM Frigidaire "electric ice box" heralded in a new "ice age,," the old ice industry collapsed The obsolete "dinosaurs" of the old ice industry (ice box manufacturers, ice gatherers, and the manufacturers of tools and equipment needed to handle large blocks of ice) faded into history. Although many lost their jobs at the time, who today would argue in favor of an icebox versus a frost-free refrigerator-freezer?

In the auto industry, General Motors today uses approximately 25,000 robots for tasks that people used to do, including spot welding, painting, machine loading, parts transfer, and assembly. Robots have replaced people in electronic assembly, mounting microchips on circuit boards. Many of the jobs replaced were dangerous, dirty and tedious. Overall, North American manufacturing companies ordered 19 percent more robots from North American robotics suppliers in 2003 than in 2002, according to new figures released by Robotic Industries Association (RIA), an industry trade group. RIA estimates that the estimated 135,000 robots now used in U.S. factories perform faster, better, and cheaper than humans ever could. In addition, using robots creates ancillary jobs, for someone must manufacture, sell, install, deliver, maintain, repair, and improve them.

During technological transitions, the difficult task is providing the education and training necessary to help people use their gifts and skills in new industries. This raises important questions about the role of education in tough economic times. Does limiting students to learning only one skill or trade help them in the end? Quality education programs should focus on training students in such a way that transitions into new emerging industries will be less costly.

Technological advances must always occur within a sound moral framework. If consistent with genuine human flourishing, humankind should embrace advances as products of human creativity rather than fear progress as a source of human suffering. Americans scapegoat foreign workers and blame them for the technological fallout resulting from change. Instead of preparing for redefined jobs and learning new skills, Americans fail to prepare for the future. They sabotage their preparedness for change by blaming the "foreigners." This type of sabotage leads to misguided policies that impede productivity improvements and innovations—the very things that make life more comfortable, safer, and healthier.

THE BUSH IMMIGRATION PLAN:
A STEP IN THE RIGHT DIRECTION

After the colossal failure of the 1986 Immigration Reform and Control Act, something had to change. Eight million undocumented immigrants later, President Bush proposed a radical amendment to the federal government's immigration policy. His plan, although imperfect, is a positive step toward helping people find jobs and fill employment gaps in the economy.

The president's proposals potentially provide legal status to millions of undocumented workers in the United States. He offers renewable three-year visas to illegal immigrants already working in the United States. Additionally, foreign applicants recently hired for jobs in the U.S. could also apply for legal status. The proposed measures essentially grant amnesty to millions of undocumented workers, allowing them— at least for the three-year period the visa is in effect—to travel freely between their homes countries and the United States. Moreover, as a legal immigrant, the worker would enjoy rights to minimum wages and due process.

Among the plan's drawbacks is the requirement making employers demonstrate the lack of Americans to fill available jobs, a prerequisite before employers may hire temporary workers from abroad. Second, immigrants could walk into an INS nightmare, because their visas automatically tie them to their employers. If illegal immigrants apply for visas, the government is able to track them. If the government fails to renew the temporary visa after three years, the immigrant could be deported. Finally, the policy is unclear about whether or not such immigrants could ever apply for permanent citizenship.

The United States is the most prosperous nation in the world with a long history of both legal and illegal immigration. For centuries, immigrants have risked their lives to find ways to use their gifts and provide for their families, often taking jobs that others do not want. In fact, massive group immigration is an ongoing fact of human history. Thomas Sowell's grand study, *Migrations and Cultures: A World View* illustrates the scope of that movement. In the past three centuries, 70 million people emigrated from Europe, with nearly 50 million coming to the United States (35 million between 1830 and 1930). Americans often view immigrants with suspicion and resentment, an attitude as old as immigration itself and unlikely to change in the future.

Nearly 4 million people emigrated from Ireland to the U.S. during the nineteenth century. Americans stereotyped the Irish as a lazy band of drunken brawlers. The Irish worked primarily in low-skilled labor jobs, and during the massive Irish immigration of the 1840s and 1850s, employers greeted hopeful Irish immigrants with signs that read "Irish Need Not Apply."

In the same century, five million Germans migrated to the United States. Large numbers became farmers and day laborers who established insular communities. These Germans, often criticized for isolating themselves from the American mainstream, conducted church services, transacted business, and published newspapers exclusively in their native tongue.

Almost 26 million people emigrated from Italy between 1876 and 1976. The early Italian immigrants took jobs that others despised at the bottom of the occupational ladder, such as sewer and sanitation workers. Italians also cordoned themselves into enclaves, their neighborhoods of 1880 to 1910 often more segregated than those of blacks.

The story is much the same for the Jewish, African, Chinese, Japanese, Mexican, and Puerto Rican immigrants over the past century. In every case, immigrants fill economic needs in their new society.

Some Americans harbor artificially inflated expectations of wages for jobs requiring few skills. Many in the unskilled labor force reject so-called menial jobs, like landscaping, food service, unskilled construction, sanitation, housekeeping, retail, and farming. Many immigrants, conversely, gladly work these jobs to establish an economic foothold in their journey to a better life.

Americans forget that "menial labor" often produces the start-up capital necessary for successive generations to achieve economic upward mobility. For example, the first Kennedy arrived in 1848 as a laborer and died a laborer. His grandsons, however, went to college and his great-grandsons became prominent American politicians.

A study by the Urban Institute shows that immigrants comprise 11 percent of the U.S. population, but 14 percent of all workers and 20 percent of low-wage workers. Without immigrant labor, the American economy suffers. Moreover, unless developing international economies grow dramatically, these numbers are only likely to expand. The president initiated decisive action to benefit a U.S. economy dependent on immigrants.

When comparing per-capita income between the U.S. and developing countries, the arrival of a wave of immigrants should come as no surprise. When 40 percent of Mexicans live below the poverty line, migrating for better opportunities makes sense, as it did for the Irish, Germans, and Italians before them.

A compassionate approach to immigration requires recognizing the inherent dignity of all people, regardless of their country of origin. The human person created for work finds life within the context of labor and family. If people desire work to provide for family and contribute to community life, then America should welcome and embrace them.

President Bush's proposal was not without problems. A major concern surrounding the plan was its seeming exoneration of illegal immigration. Granting amnesty to illegal aliens was unfair to those who have abided by the law. Changing the rules mid-game is a dangerous threat to the rule of law itself, on which American prosperity is founded.

However, the president was not faced with an ideal situation; he was faced with millions of illegal immigrants already resident in the United States, many holding down jobs. The plan sought to manage the absorption of immigrants in a way consistent with economic realities and with this nation's history as a haven for those seeking to improve their condition.

THE RISE OF THE BLACK ENTREPRENEUR:
A NEW FORCE FOR ECONOMIC AND MORAL LEADERSHIP

On May 14–18 in Nashville, Tennessee, a significant annual gathering of African Americans will occur. It will not be a meeting of high-ranking black government employees nor is it a meeting of the NAACP. Rather, this gathering is the Black Enterprise/Microsoft Entrepreneurs Conference, an important meeting of black business people. Its significance lies in the fact that the entrepreneur, not the pastor—and certainly not the politician—now typifies the future of national black political leadership.

Over the last two decades, black entrepreneurs have done more to improve the economic situation for "the black community" than any black pastor or politician. These entrepreneurs are taking the risks and building the businesses that create economic growth and prosperity. This is in stark contrast to the efforts of the Congressional Black Caucus, which has done little to encourage entrepreneurs and has limited its efforts to securing increased funding for feckless programs that harm African Americans. Sadly, many politically inclined black pastors are stuck in the rhetoric of the 1960s (and even the 1980s for that matter) speaking about need for coercive affirmative action programs and lamenting the diminished economic status of African Americans.

Since the 1960s—and even more rapidly since the 1980s—the social and economic situation for African Americans has dramatically changed. For example, most black people in America do not attend church regularly, contrary to popular perceptions. Recent data from the Barna Research Group indicate that black Americans attend church at a rate similar to that of whites. Currently, 43 percent of black people attend church on a given Sunday compared with 42 percent of whites. Moreover, according to Barna's research, 21 percent of blacks are completely un-churched compared with 32 percent of whites. Perhaps there is more equality in American than commonly supposed ... and that may not be for the better.

Despite the misperceptions disseminated about African Americans by TV and Hollywood movies, most blacks are actually members of the middle class. Furthermore, most blacks do not live in America's inner city neighborhoods; instead, nearly 40 percent of blacks live in the suburbs. The percentage of adult African Americans holding college degrees is 17 percent as compared with 20 percent of adult Americans overall.

Furthermore, it is surprising to learn that, according to research done by the Kaufman Foundation, blacks between the ages of twenty-four to thirty-five are 50 percent more likely than whites to engage in entrepreneurial activities. In other words, the most active group of entrepreneurs in American is black men and women. This reality, still unrecognized by leaders in both political parties, is producing a new and welcome leadership paradigm in the black community.

This new reality leads one to ask an important question, especially as it relates to politics: Why is there no significant black leadership in either major political party? One answer, arguably the correct one, is that leaders in both parties are tapping into political "dry wells". The future of black political leadership does not lie with the black pastor and his local political machine, oiled with government dollars. The locus of black political leadership is shifting away from the traditional black pastor and to the black entrepreneur. This reality arises from a simple fact—while the American majority does not attend church, blacks and whites alike, Americans live in a nation where everyone participates in the market as a producer or a consumer.

While politics failed in raising diverse national leadership, the marketplace has done so with amazing success. America's best kept secret is that many blacks are well-off and hold critical positions in America's largest corporations—companies like Merrill Lynch, American Express, AOL Time Warner, Citigroup, Verizon, United Parcel Service, General Electric, Morgan Stanley, to name only a few. The marketplace promotes and rewards competence, performance, and results.

Historically, the black church assumed the role of pastoral cum political leadership that produced significant gains for African Americans. Black pastors acquired significant access and power in government and business, serving as the conduit through which opportunities flowed. Such an arrangement today, however, is unnecessary because blacks hold key positions in business and government themselves. This is not to say, however, that with this shift in leadership black pastors no longer play an important role in addressing key issues—they certainly do.

The marketplace still needs the moral leadership provided by religious leaders. These days, though, most people understand that the economic improvement of the "black community" directly depends on the economic improvement of all Americans. As such, the strategies and rhetoric of past eras must fall to the wayside in favor of the new order of leadership offered by black entrepreneurs.

PART THREE

Culture

MTV'S WACK MORALITY

IN 2009, MTV ANNOUNCED the launch of "A Thin Line," a multi-year initiative aimed at stopping the spread of abuse through sexting, cyber bullying and digital dating. MTV says that the goal of the initiative is to empower America's youth to identify, respond to and block the spread of the various forms of digital harassment. While MTV's program deserves an honorable mention, the network misses the mark by ignoring its complicity in glorifying mores associated with sexting, bullying, and dating abuse, failing to promote the family, and failing to enlist religious leaders.

"A Thin Line" rolled out the same week MTV and The Associated Press released a report citing the full scope of digital abuse by teens and young adults. According to the study, 50 percent of 14-to-24-year-olds have been the target of some form of digital abuse. Thirty percent have sent or received nude photos of other young people on their cell phones or online. And 12 percent of those who have sexted have contemplated suicide, a rate four times higher than that found among those who have refrained.

During the program launch, Stephen Friedman, general manager of MTV, says "there is a very thin line between private and public, this moment and forever, love and abuse, and words and wounds. 'A Thin Line' is built to empower our audience to draw their own line between digital use and digital abuse."

While it helpfully encourages teens to report abuse, MTV seems incapable of getting to the root of the problem: namely, the cultivation of prudence that orients a teen's choices at the outset. Empowering an audi-

59

ence of teenagers is futile if their parents do not encourage the teenagers to tap into parental wisdom.

Soliciting parental wisdom regarding appropriate cell-phone usage, accountability, and navigating the social morass of adolescence is key to proper adolescent development. A parent's joy and calling is to do their best to instill moral wisdom and protect their children from evil. Sexting, bullying, and neurotic text messaging in dating relationships will remain a problem as long as teens are not aspiring to love what is good in community. The primary place to nurture children to this end is the family.

Parents themselves need to be encouraged to fulfill this responsibility. Many parents care more about their children's financial success than their character and integrity. Dr. Madeline Levine, author of *The Price of Privilege*, laments that, while many teens are academically successful and materially comfortable, they lack moral agency and the "ability to act appropriately in one's best interest." By promoting parents merely as a place to report abuse after the fact, MTV is missing a huge opportunity to enrich the public good.

MTV should do three things. First, it should empower its audience to involve parents before abuse starts instead of after the fact. MTV could do more to promote the virtues of healthy family life in its programming.

Second, cease the glorification of careless sexuality and interpersonal conflict by canceling shows celebrating the thin line between "love and abuse, and words and wounds." Programs like "Jersey Shore," "The Real World," "The Hills," and "My Super Sweet 16," glamorize greed, envy, strife, deceit, malice, gossip, slander, and arrogance. MTV's left hand profits from "thin line" programming while the right hand now condemns its own broadcasting ethos.

Third, MTV needs subversive innovation in order to broaden its partnerships. MTV's current partners include Facebook, MySpace, LoveIsRespect.org, and others, but cell-phone practices are moral issues requiring the insights of religious wisdom. Interpersonal ethics is an area begging for the time-tested expertise of religious communities. To ignore those institutions is to ignore the core foundations of civil society.

"A Thin Line" represents a new opportunity for MTV to demonstrate radical progressiveness. Instead, band-aid solutions, dealing with only the consequences, substitute for courageous moral leadership. Progressive institutions address real issues at their root causes. To be serious about confronting abuse, MTV needs to look in the mirror and support rather than undermine the adults who are trying to impart the message of human dignity to the next generation.

LESS RELIGION MEANS MORE GOVERNMENT

Soviet communism adopted Karl Marx's teaching that religion was the "opiate of the masses," which launched a campaign of bloody religious persecution. Marx misunderstood the role of religion, but years later, many communists realized that turning people away from religious life increased their dependence on government to address life's problems. The history of government coercion, derived from substituting government for religion, makes a new study citing a national decline in religious life particularly alarming to those concerned about individual freedom.

The *American Religious Identification Survey*, published by Trinity College in Hartford, Conn., reports that by 2030 one in five Americans will avow no religious commitment. The study, titled "American Nones: The Profile of the No Religion Population," reports that Americans professing no religion, or Nones, have become more mainstream and similar to the general public in marital status, education, racial and ethnic makeup and income. The Nones have increased from 8.1 percent of the U.S. adult population in 1990 to 15 percent in 2008.

According to the study, 22 percent of American 18 to 29-year-olds now self-identify as Nones. For those promoting dependency on government to handle the challenges of everyday life, as well as those who wish to take advantage of a growing market for morally bankrupt products and services, the news of declining religious life is welcome.

The increase in non-religious identification among younger generations highlights a continued shift away from active participation in one of the key social institutions that shaped this country. It comes as no surprise, then, that according to the research firm Greenberg Quinlan Rosner, voters under thirty are more liberal than all other generations. When asked about their ideology, 27 percent of those under thirty identify themselves as liberal, compared to 19 percent of baby boomers, and 17 percent of seniors. Pragmatic utilitarianism, favorable views toward a larger role for government in helping the disadvantaged, and a lack of ethical norms characterize this young segment of America's population.

The most significant difference between the religious and non-religious populations is gender. Whereas 19 percent of American men are Nones only 12 percent of American women are. The gender ratio among Nones is sixty males for every forty females.

The marketplace and society in general will both reap the consequences of numerous male Nones. As more and more men abandon the religious communities that provided solid moral formation for thousands of years, increasing demands for morally reprehensible products will explode. The breakdown of the family will follow closely behind. With consciences formed by utility, pragmatism, and sensuality, instead of virtue, one can expect to find more women subjected to the dehumanization of strip clubs, more misogynistic rap music, more adultery and divorce, more broken sexuality, more fatherlessness, more corruption in government and business, more individualism, and more loneliness.

Alexis de Tocqueville cautioned in his 1835 reflections on Democracy in America, that the pursuit of liberty without religion hurts society because it "tends to isolate [people] from one another, to concentrate every man's attention upon himself; and it lays open the soul to an inordinate love of material gratification." In fact, Tocqueville says, "the main business of religions is to purify, control, and restrain that excessive and exclusive taste for well-being which men acquire in times of equality." Religion answers the question, "Am I my brother's keeper?"

Historically, religious communities in the United States addressed the needs of local communities in ways clearly outside the scope of government. For example, as David G. Dalin writes in "The Jewish War on Poverty," between the 1820s and the Civil War, Jews laid the foundation for many charitable institutions outside the synagogue including a network of orphanages, fraternal lodges, hospitals, retirement homes, settlement houses, free-loan associations, and vocational training schools. These were also normative activities for both Protestant and Catholic religious communities on even a larger scale in communities across America before Franklin Roosevelt's New Deal.

The reported decline in religious life foreshadows the decline of virtue-driven local charities. The more Americans rely on government guidance, protection, and financial support, the more their passion to pursue good withers on the vine. When Americans surrender their lives to government control, they no longer need think for themselves. Thus, the surrender of will kills the capacity to reason and act independently. The real "opiate of the masses," it would seem, is not religion but the lack of it.

FROM CRISIS TO CREATIVE
ENTREPRENEURIAL LIBERATION

Necessity is the mother of invention, said Plato, and the truth of the proverb has been borne out once again. Necessity is generating entrepreneurial energy amid America's current economic crisis, according to a new study by the Kansas City-based Kaufman Foundation. The study reveals an increase in business startups during 2008, as the recession was taking hold. The rise is consistent with similar previous trends, such as the boomlet occurring after the tech bust of the 1990s. Throughout human history, a nation's best resource in time of crisis has been the unleashed creative and entrepreneurial spirit of its citizens.

According to the study, U.S. entrepreneurship rates increased for lowest-income-potential and middle-income-potential types of businesses from 2007 to 2008 but decreased for the highest-income-potential types of businesses. In other words, the highest growth rates were among necessity-inspired everyday Americans. The entrepreneurial spirit embedded in all human persons stirred in women and men at all levels of society.

The oldest age group—ages fifty-five to sixty-four—experienced a big increase in business-creation rates from 2007 to 2008 and, as a result, has the highest level of business creation at 0.36 percent. Among immigrants, entrepreneurial activity rates increased sharply in 2008 from 0.46 percent in 2007 to 0.53 percent in 2008, further widening the gap between immigrant and native-born rates. Even within the field of high-income type enterprises, immigrants remain more likely than U.S. natives to start businesses.

Continuing an upward trend that began in 2005, Latino entrepreneurial activity rates increased from 0.40 percent in 2007 to 0.48 percent in 2008. During the thirteen years of the study, Latinos have had the overall highest percentage increase in entrepreneurial activity: from 0.33 percent in 1996 to 0.48 percent in 2008.

Among Asian-Americans, entrepreneurial activity also increased substantially, from 0.29 percent in 2007 to 0.35 percent in 2008. The study concludes by noting that white business-creation rates increased slightly, while African-American rates slightly declined.

Looking at gender, women are experiencing faster growth in their rate of entrepreneurial activity than are men. From 2007 to 2008, men's rate increased from 0.41 percent to 0.42 percent, while the women's rate climbed from 0.20 percent to 0.24. Geographically, the states with the highest 2008 entrepreneurial activity rates were Georgia (with Atlanta leading among large cities), New Mexico, Montana, Arizona, Alaska and California. The states with the lowest entrepreneurial activity rates were Pennsylvania, Missouri, Wisconsin, West Virginia, Iowa and Ohio.

The data from the Kaufman Foundation should come as no surprise. The entrepreneurial spirit is a natural characteristic of being human. What enables free societies to recover and advance beyond poverty and economic collapse is the extent to which they liberate their citizens' entrepreneurial spirit to meet real needs freely in the long run. Nothing raises the standard of living for a society more than free people using their creativity to enhance the lives of their neighbors.

Championing the entrepreneurial spirit is not, however, a tacit affirmation of all enterprising activity. The best entrepreneurial effort enlivens virtue and orients society toward the good. Immoral forms of crisis-driven entrepreneurial activity undermine the character and integrity of the producer and the consumer. Recent schemes to defraud the vulnerable, to steal private property (subsequently resold on the black market) and to engage in human trafficking and prostitution illustrate the dark side of crisis-driven entrepreneurship.

When individuals are truly free to exercise their talents and trade the production of their labor, without oppression from tyrants or the entanglements of unnecessary government "oversight," the net effect is mutually beneficial for society as a whole. Robert Fairlie, professor of economics at the University of California, Santa Cruz and author of the Kaufman study, notes, "The continuing effects of the recession on business creation are important because entrepreneurs contribute to economic growth, innovation and job creation in the United States."

Hope abounds for economic recovery in the United States as more and more Americans use their freedom to contribute to society's benefit. More broadly, hope remains strong that people of all nations will win basic human rights, private property security, and the necessary legal protections to prove that the entrepreneurial spirit is the positive global force needed to deliver material goods to all.

ARE COMMON SENSE STUDIES NECESSARY?

The United States is so wealthy that it awards researchers millions of dollars per year to fund "important" studies that report nothing beyond common sense. Why does it take a research team of PhDs to create statistical tables that illustrate nothing more than common knowledge? The booming research study market shows that everyone, from insider politicians to new parents, quotes the latest quasi-research data as if they were quoting the Bible.

One recently released study contains the amazing finding that breathing clean air is better for one's health than breathing dirty air. The January issue of *The New England Journal of Medicine* reports that a research team from the Harvard School of Public Health and Brigham Young University examined pollution content in fifty-one U.S. cities during the 1980s and 1990s. They found that people living in cities where air pollution had declined enjoyed an increased life expectancy concomitant with increases in air quality. This is heady stuff!

The authors of the study conclude: "A reduction in exposure to ambient fine-particulate air pollution contributed to significant and measurable improvements in life expectancy in the United States."

If this case study fails to rock one's world view, perhaps the study proving that high school dropouts are likelier to demonstrate dependence instead independence and generally lead, less productive lives will be an epiphany? According to a "groundbreaking" study conducted by The Economics Center for Education & Research at the University of Cincinnati, at the request of the Ohio Alliance of Public Charter Schools (OAPCS), on average, each student failing to graduate from high school will end up costing Ohio taxpayers $3,909 per year from age 16 to 64, or about $191,500 over a lifetime. Based on this analysis, the cost to taxpayers of the 40,000 young people who drop out of school each year in Ohio is more than $156 million annually.

Dropouts are at higher risk for unemployment, underemployment and criminal behavior resulting in expensive incarceration, according to the study. They pay less in state and local taxes and are much more dependent on public assistance such as welfare payments, housing subsidies, food stamps, unemployment benefits and Medicare and Medicaid—in addition to the immeasurable human misery that results from dropouts' inability to participate successfully in the economy.

And the following research is a real eye opener—according to a new study, the virginity pledges adolescents make are not lasting! This is groundbreaking news! Virginity pledges alone do not decrease teenagers' sexual behavior, says a report in the January issue of *Pediatrics*.

Health researcher Janet Elise Rosenbaum of Johns Hopkins Bloomberg School of Public Health found that abstinence pledges were 10 percent less likely than non-pledges to use condoms or any form of birth control. Using data from a 1996 National Longitudinal Study of Adolescent Health, Rosenbaum compared the sexual behaviors of 289 teenagers who reported taking a verbal or written virginity pledge with 645 non-pledges sharing similar religious or conservative views, according to K. Aleisha Fetters of Medill Reports. "Five years after their pledges, the two groups did not differ in rates of premarital sex, sexually transmitted infections or oral or anal sex practices."

Rosenbaum also found that five years after taking their pledges, 82 percent of pledges denied having taken them. Public pledges, in large groups, often function like New Year's resolutions. To make matters worse, teenagers who took a virginity pledge and had sex were less likely to use condoms. The real question should be why people believed that teenagers pledging steadfast sexual abstinence, outside of broader and deeper commitments to moral virtue, could maintain their resolve. Perhaps raging hormones, peer pressure, and popular culture overcame wobbly moral virtue. . . hard to believe. Someone needs to do a study on the adults who came up with the virginity pledge—could belief in the pledge, the Tooth Fairy, and flying pigs correlate somehow?

In the end, many of these researchers earn university tenure and awards for discovering things that generations of parents have taught their children—for example, toxins are toxic, education is vital for making a contribution to society and supporting oneself and one's family, and sexuality divorced from a strong moral code restricting it to marriage is aimless and damaging.

In today's meritocracy, costly university studies substitute for time-tested guidance from the elder generation. Even professionals have come to rely on these studies for public credibility. They permit commentators and essayists to say with authority, "See, I told you so." As a result, people pay for insight that they could receive free from clergy, older family members, and other sources of wisdom. In the end, these studies demonstrate, as ancient wisdom states, "What has been will be again, what has been done will be done again; there is nothing new under the sun."

GREENBOOZLED

Being "green" is the new cool. "Green Christmas" and toy purchases from Greentoys.com this season will advertise to one's friends and relatives that one cares about the environment. However, environmentalists are balking. They say that too many companies are claiming to be green and thus are "greenwashing" everything.

Greenpeace describes greenwashing as the act of misleading consumers regarding the environmental practices of a company or the environmental benefits of a product or service. The deeper irony is that greenwashing was the original tactic many environmentalists used to manipulate the public into adopting practices that actually do not sustain the environment. An alternate term for greenwashing would be greenboozled.

One of the unintended consequences of a greenwashing environmental rhetoric is that being green is now fashionable—a fad. Marketing departments discovered how easy it is to sell products to people who want to feel good about their consumption problem. Greenwashing works because most Americans do not think about negative spillover effects, environmental processes, long-term effects on the poor, or the economic implications of allegedly environment-friendly proposals. Simply saying something is green is enough for many people. Who cares if it is true or if it works? People are satisfied with the arbitrary labeling.

Environmentalists do not want the public to believe the green claims coming from large corporations in manufacturing and energy production, but these are the same people who greenwashed the public into believing that ethanol is environmentally better than gasoline, that recycling improves the environment, and many other such greenwashed untruths. Stewardship of the environment is yet another area furnishing evidence that ethical integrity is critical to effective action. Consumers need more honesty and less exaggeration.

The National Ethanol Vehicle Coalition (NEVC), the nation's primary advocacy group promoting the use of E85 fuel (85 percent ethanol fuel, 15 percent gasoline) as a form of alternative transportation fuel, was positioned to greenwash Americans until Dr. Mark Z. Jacobson of Stanford University and other researchers revealed the truth about E85 fuel. In a 2007 study, Jacobson demonstrated that ethanol is just as bad for the environment as gasoline.

Because of its effects on the ozone, future E85 may be a greater over-all public health risk than gasoline. In fact, if America moves toward the proposed E85 fuel goals, this change may increase ozone-related mortality, hospitalization, and asthma by 4 percent in the United States as a whole relative to 100 percent gasoline use. Jacobson and others confidently concluded only that E85 is unlikely to improve air quality over future gasoline vehicles. Unburned ethanol emissions from E85 may result in a global-scale source of acetaldehyde greater than that caused by direct emissions. Why is the NEVC still greenboozling the American public?

Perhaps the greatest greenwash of all is the mythology surrounding the environmental benefits of recycling. In reality, the only real benefi-ciaries of the recycling movement are environmental groups and recy-cling companies. According to Progressive Investor, from 1968 to 2008, the recycling industry grew from $4.6 billion in annual sales to roughly $236 billion.

However, William McDonough and Michael Braungart, authors of *Cradle to Cradle*, employ logic coupled with hard data to demonstrate that the energy, chemicals, and toxins used in the recycling process cre-ate hazardous products and environmental waste equal to the original production. This is true in part because Americans do not manufacture products to be recycled at the outset. As such, the waste produced by putting metals, plastics, and paper through the recycling processes yields no real environmental gain.

As McDonough and Braungart point out, the products Americans believe they are "recycling" are actually "downcycled"—when Americans recycle metals, plastics, and paper, these products are turned into lower quality materials For example, paper requires extensive bleaching and other chemicals to make it white again for reuse, resulting in a mixture of chemicals, pulp, and at times, toxic inks.

Why, then, does the National Recycling Coalition encourage en-vironmentally harmful processes and recycled products that eventually end up in landfills anyway? There is nothing wrong with recycling as an industry but the public should look askance at the claims that recycling helps the environment.

Any dialogue about the environment requires honest disclosure of the facts and acknowledging that good intentions do not make good policy. Truthfulness in environmentalism is a call to weigh the facts, prioritize the needs of the poor, and keep government bureaucrats from instituting policy based on greenboozling rhetoric. Effectively meeting the needs of human welfare and responsibly caring for the environment requires telling the unvarnished truth.

WHO'S TO BLAME FOR CHUBBY CHILDREN?

Are America's children overweight because of advertising? A new study suggests that banning fast food ads would reduce the number of overweight children ages three to eleven by 18 percent and would reduce the number of overweight adolescents ages twelve to eighteen by 14 percent. However, common sense—something often missing from research reports and very underrated in America today—would suggest that good parenting remains the single most important variable in child obesity.

Once upon a time, children begged for things that they had neither the maturity nor the discernment to resist. Their parents simply replied, "No." This new study reveals more about the deterioration of the American family than the likely effectiveness of advertising censorship. In reality, television commercials do not make kids fat but parents surely can. (Aside from the question of genetic predisposition to obesity, the author means to imply no blame to those who are blameless.) Children learn good or bad eating habits actively, through parental oversight, or passively, through parental neglect.

Of course, precocious toddlers and young children, after watching tempting fast food ads on TV, hop in their cars, drive to the nearest fast food restaurant, and blow their hard-earned paychecks on grotesquely big grease burgers and gargantuan orders of fries. In this alternate bizarre universe, children reach puberty and go hog-wild! They embrace a revised version of the five food groups—sugar, salt, caffeine, fat, and fat. Poof! The evil junk food fairy erases all of the good eating habits these teenagers learned as children. As in every fairy tale, the parents' role is diminished or absent and the victimized children exist as plot devices to move the story along.

Researchers excluded any family related statistics in their data analysis, which skewed the results of the study. They conducted their research in a vacuum divorced from reality. Although researchers promulgate advertising's hypnotic control over children, a healthy family life affects a child's choices far more profoundly than any media influence. In its narrow focus on media, the study failed to ask other critical questions. This study is a fairy tale.

Do obese children come from homes in which parents and children do not share regular family meals? Results from a study published in *Obesity Research* show that children who regularly eat with other family members are 15 percent less likely to be overweight compared to those who never or only sometimes eat dinner with another family member. In addition, the more frequently children ate dinner with their families, the less likely they were to be overweight.

Internationally, nutrition experts now recognize that the most effective ways to decrease childhood obesity are daily family meals coupled with greater parental influence on children's food options.

In October, participants at the Children's Nutrition Research Centre conference in Brisbane, Australia, heard about a two-year health study showing parents and children who started a healthy food program lost more weight than those who focused solely on exercise. The survey by Clare Collins, a health school professor at the University of Newcastle, examined 165 obese children aged five to nine. It underlined the fact that parents were still the biggest influence on child nutritional health. "The most important thing you can do for your kids is to sit down at the table as a family," she said.

A July study by the American Medical Association recommends that families concerned with combating childhood obesity, "limit consumption of sweetened beverages and fast food, limit screen time, engage in physical activity for at least sixty minutes per day," and hold family meals on "most, and preferably all, days of the week."

Divorced and single parent families, understandably in light of the time challenges they face, often see fast food as an easier option. Children raised by single parents are more likely to be overweight than those in two-parent families, according to a national study published in the *International Journal of Obesity*. Researchers studied more than 7,000 children aged seven to eleven and found that those raised by one parent were 40 percent more likely to be overweight.

Adults in general may share blame, however, because of their own poor eating habits. Childhood obesity rates essentially mirror obesity rates among adults. The U.S. Centers for Disease Control and Prevention (CDC) estimates that overweight rates are 13.9 percent of children age two to five, 18.8 percent of those age six to eleven, and more than 17 percent of those age twelve to nineteen. The most recent CDC data reveals that among adult men the prevalence of obesity was 33.3 percent, and 35.3 percent among women.

There is an ancient proverb, "Train a child in the way he should go, and when he is old he will not turn from it." Banning advertising will have no effect on the fact that childhood obesity is most often a function of the nature of the relationships of those closest to them, the people called parents.

JOHN EDWARDS IS THE REAL WORLD

Why are Americans shocked to learn that John Edwards committed adultery and lied about it? People think they know their neighbors, friends, and families, but little do they really know. Adulterous promiscuity is the American way—it ranks right up there with baseball and apple pie.

The market responds accordingly. Every night, primetime television depicts non-marital sex as preferable to the beauty of a good marriage. According to a new report by the Parents Television Council, "across the broadcast networks, verbal references to non-marital sex outnumbered references to sex in the context of marriage by nearly 3-to-1; and scenes depicting or implying sex between non-married partners outnumbered scenes depicting or implying sex between married partners by a ratio of nearly 4-to-1."

Americans cannot look away from broadcasts recounting every salacious detail of every illicit affair. They glue themselves to their TVs to soak up every sordid image America cannot have it both ways. This country cannot tolerate these dehumanizing entertainments, reward the sponsors of these shows with consumer dollars, and then feign outrage when American leaders act like reality show stars parading their bad behavior in front of an avid audience.

Advertising revenue and viewer ratings manifest the market's celebration of promiscuous, irresponsible non-marital sexuality by supporting programs that normalize the infidelity of John Edwards, Jesse Jackson, Bill Clinton, Newt Gingrich, Elliot Spitzer, and many others—including friends, family, and neighbors. Many Americans seem to think that what matters are not the acts of destroying humanity through sexual immorality, wrecking a marriage, or emotionally scarring children—getting caught *in flagrante delicto*, red-handed and red-faced is the problem.

What televisions programs fail to depict, however, is the fact that in the real world promiscuous sexuality and adultery produce deep, lasting pain for all parties involved, especially the devastated children whose parents commit this sin.

John Edwards perfectly describes the transition, saying that his growing fame and power "fed a self-focus, an egotism, a narcissism that leads you to believe that you can do whatever you want and you're invisible and there will be no consequences . . . and nothing could be further from the truth." This should serve as a warning to all Americans.

The tempting mix of sex, money, and power make a deadly cocktail of self-destruction. An ancient proverb states, "your sins will find you out." It is a chilling fact that truth eventually exposes deception. It is simply how the world works.

When asked why he initially denied the allegations, Edwards commented that he "did not want the public to know what [he] had done." Why are commentators recoiling because Edwards lied about the affair? If a person commits adultery in the first place—massive betrayal of trust—why would the same kind of person not lie about it in public?

Once again, Americans expose their lack of moral values, the necessary character formation concomitant with professional success. Americans do not demand it of their leaders because Americans do not demand it of themselves. Having the right ideology or professional achievements are far more important than cultivating character and virtue. Leaders without character ultimately misuse economic, political, social relationships in ways that eventually hurt people.

In the decades to come, the American social narrative will tell more stories like this because Americans are not inculcating virtue in children. Are parents today raising children to be women and men of prudence, courage, justice, and self-control? Or are they raising children who will be self-focused, egotistical, narcissistic, believing they are invincible and morally accountable to no one? That is, "successful," but lacking integrity.

Today's American family, with its high rate of divorce, abuse, relational brokenness, poor media content preferences, success worship, and materialism, grooms its children to become the type of adults who will one day be on television publicly admitting to impropriety. Americans get the leaders they deserve because these leaders represent what the people truly value.

HIP HOP'S DELUSIONAL GOD-TALK

When Lil' Wayne approached the microphone at the 2008 BET Awards saying, "I am nothing without God, baby! I just want to say thank God, thank my family and thank Universal." To what god was he paying homage? Does he worship some ancient god named "Misogyny?" There is a serious disconnect in the hip-hop community that allows rappers to evoke the name of God in thanks while producing music that celebrates evil.

The profound disconnect may be explained, in part, by a new study released by Radio One and Yankelovich, a Chapel Hill-based research firm. The new study, the most comprehensive in decades including blacks ranging in age from thirteen to seventy-four, reveals that while 83 percent of blacks call themselves Christians, only 41 percent attend church at least once a week. Even worse, among black men, 47 percent say they are not as religious as their parents (36 percent of black women confess the same).

For black teens, 86 percent say that they trust God to take care of things and 46 percent believe that they are not as religious as their parents. Most black teens see God as a stopgap measure only. This is why Lil' Wayne receives applause, even though he raps about the sadistic treatment of women to an audience full of deistic blacks.

Deism is a movement forged in the seventeenth and eighteenth centuries in England proffering the idea that God created the world but has no interest in intervening in the world's present functioning, including ethical matters. Hip Hop's deism allows Lil' Wayne to produce disgusting songs like "Lollipop" and receive the "Viewers Choice" award while attributing his success to God.

Perhaps it would have been more accurate for Lil' Wayne to thank the convergence of all of the forces of evil that allow lyrics like "Shawty wanna lic-lic-lic-lick me/Like a lollipop" to be praised by viewers. Universal's sponsorship of Lil' Wayne's music is but one indication of the fact that hip-hop has become big business. "Lollipop" recently hit number one on the "Billboard Hot 100 Top 10" list and the album, "Tha Carter III" now debuts at number one among Billboard's "Top 40 Albums."

Pure evil celebrates music that maligns the dignity of women and men. In the song, "Don't Get It," Lil' Wayne, while harshly criticizing the Rev. Al Sharpton, laments being misunderstood. Lil' Wayne is indeed hard to understand: he seems to be a confused deist, at best, with no desire to integrate, in his music, gratitude to God with the demands of human dignity, justice, and love.

Lil' Wayne's thanking God is equivalent to a strip club patron thanking God for providing women to objectify and dehumanize, or a prostitute thanking God that she has the ability to destroy her dignity to pay bills. Some "successes," correctly attributable to social moral decay and the unchecked spread of evil, cannot be purified by a passing mention of "God." With its culture-rotting messages, much of hip-hop exemplifies the kind of enterprise that does not credit the market that gave birth to it.

One should not be too surprised by the juxtaposition of God talk with dehumanizing rap lyrics when nearly half of all black men are not as religious as their partly religious parents and most blacks no longer attend church—the black community's historic source of moral formation.

The internet lit up in late June when rapper Ice-T attacked Soulja Boy saying that he "single-handedly killed hip hop" with his "garbage" song "Superman." One might add that the empty God talk in hip-hop today is single-handedly perverting the relationship between God and virtue for an audience of blacks who are increasingly unchurched and uncommitted to a life in pursuit of the good.

Ice-T makes a distinction between "good hip hop" and "whack hip hop" in his warranted attack of Soulja Boy's song, but a better distinction would separate virtue-building hip-hop from virtue-destroying hip-hop. The genre's deistic language exposes just how confused and disconnected the hip-hop generation is from the black church platform on which it stands, enjoying its freedom to dishonor the black experience in America.

STEVE HARVEY OFFERS HOPE FOR BLACK RADIO

As black history month comes to a close, it is worth drawing attention to bright spots in black culture. One is comedian Steve Harvey's morning radio show. Harvey brings challenging commentary on aspects of black life using critical humor. Together with other solid black radio programs, Harvey's show renews hope that African-Americans will successfully address the moral and socio-economic ills troubling their communities.

Unlike many black radio personalities, Harvey is not afraid to call out ignorance. The morning show gained attention several months ago when Harvey made a public declaration that he would never play misogynistic music that degrades black women. This type of direct, on-air leadership will help put a dent in a genre of music that is rending the social fabric of society.

For example, one of the most pathetic songs in popular hip last year was Soulja Boy's song "Crank Dat." With lyrics that would cause the Rev. Dr. Martin Luther King to turn in his grave, Harvey made a point not only to name the immorality in the song but also to encourage others to think hard about the content of putrid music represented by artists like Soulja Boy.

The content and lyrics of "Crank Dat" are too sordid to describe here, but sorrowfully the song was number 21 on Rolling Stone's list of the "100 Best Songs of 2007." It was the 2007 number one music video on the now morally bankrupt BET (Black Entertainment Television), and it received a Grammy nomination for "Best Rap Song" in 2007.

Although the song peaked in America at number one, in New Zealand's "Top Forty Chart" at number two, and in the United Kingdom's "R&B Singles Chart" at number one, Harvey did not allow market success to trump his moral principles.

When trying to reach black America, radio remains an extremely powerful medium. A new report by Arbitron, a media and marketing research firm, confirms the social leverage of black radio. "Black Radio Today" calculates that more than 1,100 of America's 13,800 radio stations are black-formatted. The report also says that radio is a medium of steady popularity among the nation's more than 22 million black Americans, ages eighteen and over. Harvey's show airs in nearly sixty markets, including many of the top ten: Los Angeles, Chicago, Dallas, Philadelphia, Washington, D.C. and Detroit.

While Harvey does a good job speaking about morals, promoting fidelity in relationships, providing inspirational content (even playing gospel music at times), this is only a drop in the bucket. All black radio shows could do more to promote the virtues of good marriages. The lack of sustainable marriages is one of the key impediments to black social and economic progress. As long as women and children lack life-long commitments with moral men, America will continue to see aggravated cycles of sexual irresponsibility, juvenile delinquency, poverty, welfare dependence, poor health care, and substandard education.

Harvey and other nationally syndicated radio personalities should also rally hip-hop and pop radio show hosts and DJs in declaring a moratorium on the distribution of music that sabotages human dignity. They could agree to promote only music with positive virtues. By airing negative, destructive music, broadcasters tacitly support irresponsible artists and their wicked message. Radio personalities are an important variable in the popular music matrix, an area begging for moral leadership.

Harvey recently reminded his audience, "The best way to start your day is to give honor to God." Courageous leadership like this confirms Harvey's ability to use radio as a medium for human flourishing instead of a vehicle for ignorance and immorality.

OBVIOUSLY, SPORTS DO NOT BUILD CHARACTER

The old adage, "Sports builds character," requires a new critical interpretation these days. Why are so many professional athletes, who have spent their entire lives in organized sports, masters at cheating, serial adultery, drunkenness, compulsive gambling, drug abuse, and thuggish fighting (to name just a few of the vices)? The truth is that sports no more builds character than attending Clemson University football games qualifies one to replace Tommy Bowden as head coach.

Character is synonymous with moral excellence, in other words, a life characterized by prudence, fortitude, self-discipline, and humility in pursuit of what is good.

University of Colorado sociologist Dr. Jay Coakley, in his book, *Sports in Society*, explains that people mistakenly believe that sports builds character for two reasons. First, they wrongly assume that all athletes have the same experiences in all organized sports. Secondly, they wrongly assume organized sports provide unique learning experiences that are not available from any other activities.

Unfortunately, whatever character-building potential may exist in the world of athletics often takes a back seat to financial profiting devoid of moral constraints. Increasing ticket sales, advertising revenue and winning, by any means necessary, are more important in professional sports than the character of the worshipped, carefully cultivated athletes. The world of professional sports is an inhumane system.

Michael Vick is only the latest and most sensational example. Vick has possibly ruined his career after pleading guilty to federal dog fighting conspiracy charges. Apparently, no one ever told Michael Vick that dog fighting is illegal, vicious, immoral, and cruel. Why would he participate in this criminal blood sport when he had it all? Why would Vick stupidly risk a $130 million NFL contract? The simple explanation that Vick's managers, agents, and coaches likely viewed him less as a person worthy of dignity and more as an "it," a mere commodity, during his formative football years cannot totally explain his behavior. Nevertheless, this pervasive attitude certainly contributed to his downfall.

Did sports build the character of Travis Henry? In 2007, a judge ordered the Denver Broncos running back to pay $3,000 a month for an Atlanta-area boy he fathered out of wedlock three years ago. Henry, 28, reportedly fathered nine children with nine different women in at least four states. In the Georgia case, Superior Court Judge Clarence Seeliger wrote that Henry also displayed "bad judgment in his spending habits," dropping $100,000 for a car and $146,000 for jewelry.

College athletes fare no better. The Benedict-Crosset Study of sexual assaults at thirty major Division I universities reports that athletes commit one out of every three college sexual assaults. The three-year study demonstrates that while male student-athletes comprise 3.3 percent of the college population, they represent 19 percent of sexual assault perpetrators and 35 percent of domestic violence perpetrators. In 2006, Duke University's lacrosse team got drunk, hired and allegedly assaulted some strippers, and made the front-page news. Rape, violent crimes, and adultery—these headlines reveal the seedy underbelly of amateur and professional sports.

Blood doping allegations sullied this year's Tour De France. T-Mobile sponsored competitor Patrick Sinkewitz, 26, faces a possible two-year ban and restitution charges of a year's salary, estimated to be $684,000, for a doping violation. Michael Waltrip, a two-time Daytona 500 winner, lost two key members of his pit crew in February when NASCAR penalized his team for using a fuel additive, NASCAR's biggest cheating scandal to date.

Hypocrisy blares like Ohio State's marching band when America expresses outrage at professional athletes' lack of character. Athletes are merely displaying the character of the adults who nurtured them. School-age athletes live in an adult world and pattern their behavior on their role models, role models who are masters at cheating, gambling, violence, serial adultery, lying, drunkenness, drug abuse, and misogyny. "Bad company corrupts good character" is such compelling ancient Greek wisdom that it is quoted in the Bible (1 Corinthians 15:33). By the time many young athletes become "professionals," they have already adopted the dissolute values learned in the company of malformed adults.

Sports do not build character in young people but virtuous adults do. In one sense youth sport is simply a medium for adult mentoring within the context of challenging, competitive situations. Character is bestowed—or not—from one generation to another.

Until adults in the world of sports are willing to commit their own lives to virtuous character, until they are willing to pair a valid desire to make money with an equally powerful concern for the true welfare of athletes, the cycle of young "professional" adults ruining their lives will continue. In athletics as elsewhere, people reap what they sow.

VIRGINIA TECH SHOOTING REVEALS
AMERICA'S NEW 'AT RISK' GROUP

As Virginia Tech students limp through the rest of the spring semester, America ponders its exposed imperfections. Free markets have given Americans an unprecedented level of wealth but prosperity, detached from a commitment to human dignity, does not ensure social harmony. Sadly, the perpetrators in the Virginia Tech and Columbine tragedies shared a deep sense of alienation, isolation, marginalization, and victimization by the mainstream and shared a hatred for the children of affluence. Mounting evidence indicates that America faces a new type of crime: educated, middle-class children represent a new "at risk" group, as both perpetrators and victims of peer-related violence.

The gravity of both the Columbine and Virginia Tech shootings reveal the pain of America's new at-risk population of middle-class youth. Clinical psychologist Dr. Madeline Levine, author of *The Price of Privilege*, points out that America's new at risk young people are preteens and teens from affluent, well-educated families. "In spite of their economic and social advantages, they experience among the highest rates of depression, substance abuse, anxiety disorders, somatic complaints, and unhappiness of any group of children in this country," writes Dr. Levine.

In 1997, after five long years of economic struggle, the family of Virginia Tech mass murderer Seung-Hui Cho moved into Centreville, Virginia, a Washington, D.C. suburb. A city with a median household income is $71,232—part of Fairfax County, a locality with the nation's fifth highest median household income according to the U.S. Census Bureau. Cho spent his formative years surrounded by children of privilege while his family struggled.

In Cho's disturbed mind, these murders were associated, in part, with a profound, narcissistic feeling of alienation and resentment toward an unidentified privileged "you": "You have never felt a single ounce of pain your whole life.\.\. Your Mercedes weren't enough, you brats. Your golden necklaces weren't enough, you snobs. Your trust funds wasn't enough.\.\.Those weren't enough to fulfill your hedonistic needs. You had everything."

The resentment of children of privilege has taken on a different shape with Generation Y, those born after 1978. In previous generations, the rich, beautiful youths would have been envied and hated from afar. Young people today act out their own self-loathing by committing personal and random acts of violence against the "in" crowd. Some might argue that this resentment is encouraged by television shows such as MTV's "Laguna Beach", "Made," and "Maui Fever," where being "hot" and having unlimited resources are paraded as the best possible way to live. Do shows like this stir up inferior feelings and resentment among the non-hot, non-wealthy, non-cool youths—i.e., regular people—because they will never be good enough?

Representing the shooter's family, Sun-Kyung Cho, his Princeton University-educated sister said, "My brother was quiet and reserved, yet struggled to fit in. We never could have envisioned that he was capable of so much violence."

Children of privilege are exhibiting unexpectedly high rates of emotional problems beginning in junior high school and accelerating through adolescence. If depressed, struggling adolescents can maintain high academic performance, their emotional and mental health problems often remain unaddressed. Although Cho's intellect landed him in honors courses in high school, his teachers and counselors overlooked Cho's fragile mental state. More than half of all depressed teens suffer recurring bouts of depression within five years of the initial episode and demonstrate an elevated risk of depression, poor social skills, increased risk of suicide attempts, and potential psychiatric hospitalization, according to Levine.

Many parents wrongly assume that high academic performance alone is the gold standard for emotional, psychological, or spiritual health. This concept of a successful student falls apart in the face of reality. Maybe the most successful kids are not the ones merely with good grades but those with a virtuous self-efficacy: the belief that they can successfully make the world a better place regardless of their being "cool," "hot," or materially comfortable.

All such speculation is limited. Perhaps when all the blaming and theorizing fail to conclusively answer the question, "Why?", one must view evil behavior not only in terms of mental health, but also within the context of spiritual and moral maturity. Garrett Evans, who survived being shot by Cho, said, "An evil spirit was going through that boy, I could feel it."

Everyone wonders how perpetrators like Cho Seung-Hui "fall through the cracks." Maybe the cracks never existed in the first place. Perhaps the failure lies in not recognizing high-risk children and young adults like Cho. Parents, teachers, and pastors fail to see the despair and potential violence simmering beneath the surface of the bright but quietly desperate academic achiever, the social misfit with good grades. 'Leaving no child behind' may have less to do with academic and extracurricular performance, and more to do with nurturing emotional, social, psychological, and spiritual health.

GHETTO CRACKER: THE HIP HOP 'SELL OUT'

What does it mean for a black person to "sell out"? Colin Powell, Condoleezza Rice, Tiger Woods and many more, carry the label "sell outs," accused of "acting white" because they speak understandable English, pursue learning and lead racially integrated lives. What is overlooked, however, is that much of the hip-hop and rap world represents a different form of "acting white" and "selling out." That is, hip-hop culture can be traced to the urbanization of the southern "redneck," or to use the more socially offensive term, "cracker" culture of the past.

Thomas Sowell, in his latest book, *Black Rednecks and White Liberals*, points out that urban black culture, as understood today, shares striking similarities to the Cracker culture of the Old South. As rustic English immigrants settled and populated America's south, their crude, unsophisticated culture became the societal norm. In the antebellum Old South, about 90 percent of U.S. blacks lived the Southern lowbrow lifestyle, marinating in the Cracker culture. When blacks migrated into major northern cities, beginning in the early twentieth century, Sowell argues that they brought redneck culture with them.

Sowell highlights the dominant social, moral, and cultural Southern redneck traits, characteristics previously expounded by Grady McWhiney in *Cracker Culture: Celtic Ways in the Old South*. The Cracker proclivities include aversion to work, violent tendencies disdain for education, sexual promiscuity, short-term thinking, drunkenness, lack of initiative, thrill seeking, and wild music and dance. Rednecks were prickly natured roosters with an overblown dramatic sense of self-importance and little self-control. They were the precursors of today's "bling-bling" mentality.

This "cracker" ethos of the past transferred seamlessly into the hip-hop world with reckless abandon. When black youths call studious blacks "white" or scold other black youths for sounding "white," they adopt a ghetto cracker mentality. Only a ghetto cracker would ridicule the pursuit of education, the speaking of correct English, and working hard. They boast of violent activities, sexual promiscuity, and "gettin' high and drunk," "acting a fool up in da' club," or bumping and grinding on the dance floor. The ghetto cracker celebrates being out of control and spending money instead of saving and investing.

Being a ghetto cracker, regardless of race, means pursuing a life-style of self-sabotage that undermines human dignity and despising the moral undergirding of a civil society. Selling out one's dignity and future to regressive moral standards is the way of the ghetto cracker.

Hip-hop magazines like *Vibe*, *The Source*, and *XXL* celebrate the ghetto cracker lifestyle. The July issue of *Vibe* glorifies the strip-club habitués, rappers the Ying Yang Twins, for example. The magazine lay-out exalts the tough, misogynist gangsta persona—the photo of rapper Pitbul posing with his toddler son in front of two naked women painted red exemplifies the publication's depraved slant. The repugnant advertising, feature, and editorial content reflect the basest human proclivities. Sex and violence sell.

An alternative vision of black American culture exists, however, that recognizes the dual values of moral and economic responsibility. The July issue of *Black Enterprise* magazine celebrates living wisely—it eschews promoting false and divisive racial dichotomies. Instead, the glossy pages feature articles about investment strategies, starting businesses, homeownership, and a profile of black astrophysicist Neil Tyson, and a 1991 PhD recipient from Columbia University. Sophisticated, well laid out ads promote the Harlem Book Fair, the American Black Film Festival, and Morehouse College. Hard work, pursuing education, the virtues of prudence, integrity, self-discipline, humility, and the advantages of marriage and family all weave the fabric of life celebrated in this alternative expression of the black community.

This is not "selling out"; it is "buying in." Buying in to the fact that authentic blackness is not being a ghetto cracker. Buying in embraces a worldview that understands our common human nature and what it means to live in a way that is truly fulfilling—a worldview that promotes dignity, work, marriage, family, and healthy community. The real sell-out is the one who urbanizes counterproductive moral values and behaviors. People like Russell Simons, Puff Daddy, 50 Cent, the Ying Yang Twins, and others encourage minorities to adopt the attitudes of the Southern, redneck cracker culture of the past while claiming authentic blackness. Being a chocolate covered antebellum redneck of yesteryear is not being "black"; it is simply "selling out" disguised as hip-hop.

THE FREE AND EASY CHARITY OF THE 'ONE CAMPAIGN'

The One Campaign, an advocacy group lobbying to direct an additional 1 percent of the U.S. budget toward foreign aid, admirably seeks to mobilize Americans to address the AIDS crisis and extreme poverty. The campaign attracted the support of prominent evangelical leaders, like Rick Warren, a large following of activist celebrities, including Bono, and several Christian artists. Now, as the leading industrial nations stand poised to forgive $40 billion in debt from the world's poorest countries at next month's G8 summit, the One Campaign hails the move as a significant victory for the world's poor.

Yet the One Campaign, founded by a group of international charities and NGOs, is fundamentally flawed—flawed because it demands $25 billion from the U.S. government to achieve this goal. The One Campaign asks Christians to respond in ways inconsistent with Jesus' teaching. The Bible never asks individuals and churches to appeal to government to help those in need; the Bible, however, does urge church member to exercise the virtue of charity.

Why appeal to the government when the church is a far better resource? John L. and Sylvia Ronsvalle, authors of "The State of Church Giving Through 2001," note that if American Christians gave 10 percent of their income to support the work of the church, this tithing would provide $143 billion to equip the church to fulfill its calling. Asking for a measly $25 billion seems absurd when American churches have more money to support directly and effectively the private groups charged with addressing urgent needs. The church-based approach allows governments to allocate their funds for building infrastructure and securing peace and justice.

In the Sermon on the Mount, Jesus exhorts his followers that they—not government—are "the light of the world." Moreover, when giving to the needy, Christians should refrain from "practicing piety before men in order to be noticed." Yet the One Campaign somehow enticed Christians like Michael W. Smith, Jars of Clay, the Newsboys, Switchfoot, and others, to endorse prominently displayed pictures of their piety on the Campaign's website.

Christian workers for centuries have responded to God's call to "seek justice" (Isaiah 1:17) and to love their neighbor (Matthew 22:39). Christians have seen it as their responsibility to extend sacrificial love to those in need by seeking justice, rebuking those who are evil, fighting on behalf of the weak, embracing those who are mistreated, and promoting freedom for all. The Samaritan story proposes to rally the church, not government.

Even black liberation theologians appeal to action modeled after the ministry of Jesus. James Cone, Distinguished Professor of Systematic Theology at Union Theological Seminary, believes that Christians are to "join the cause of the oppressed in the fight for justice." Authentic Christian identity is found when Christians change their lifestyles to effect real change. "Christians fight not for humanity in general," he says, "but for themselves and out of love for concrete human beings."

In contrast, the One Campaign says nothing about sacrificial love or the promotion of human dignity. What's more, it promotes a depersonalized and sterile form of help characteristic of the secular appeal to radical individualism.

Interestingly, the campaign does not encourage sacrificial living by curbing purchases of music CDs or movies, in order to give more personal resources to help the poor, the sick, and the oppressed. Americans could have donated the $12.2 billion spent on music in 2004 to fight poverty and AIDS. In fact, in 2004 alone, U.S. consumers spent $21.2 billion on DVD sales and rentals, $9.9 billion on video games, $14.6 billion on chocolate, $9.4 billion at the box office, and $2.8 billion North American revenue from concert tickets. Besides, does anyone really need to go to a U2 or Jars of Clay concert?

Personal sacrifice for the sake of the poor could mean a little less wealth and little less fame for the wealthy and famous entertainers behind the One Campaign. However, that might not be a bad thing, since the music stars currently use their influence to make demands on how the government should use other people's money.

"One by one" is the campaign's mantra. A far superior campaign for these artists to support is the "one by one" personal virtue of charity that God calls Christians to enact through the church and other faith-based organizations. Much more could be accomplished by bypassing the bureaucratic inefficiencies of government, freeing it to do other good things, and giving a portion of the $143 billion to those agencies that do charity better than government ever could.

CANDY SHOPPING—RAP'S DEHUMANIZING MESSAGE

The good thing about the market is that it efficiently provides the goods that people want. The bad thing about the market is that it does the same thing. Therefore, it is imperative for a free market system to nest safely within a moral culture, one concerned with protecting human dignity and promoting true human flourishing. Much of today's most popular rap music (departing from rap's origins), is a putrid cesspool of lyrics glorifying materialism ("bling bling") and depicting distorted carica-tures of authentic masculinity and femininity.

Contrary to what some may believe, rap is not a genre peculiar to a black subculture: *The Boston Globe* reports that over 70 percent of all rap music purchases are by white suburban youth. Rap and hip-hop music overall has a listening audience that is 75 percent non-black.

Reference to women as objects of men's sexual fulfillment and the glorification of subhuman lifestyles permeate this diverse world of rap music. Artist 50 Cent in a recent number one hit, "Candy Shop," sings to a woman that he is going to take her to a candy shop to let her "lick the lollipop." He then offers to have random sex with her "in the hotel or in the back of the rental." When they meet "it's like a race who can get undressed quicker."

Noted rap star The Game performs a top hit, "How We Do," boast-ing that he and his friends "act a fool while we up in da' club." The Game longs to find the right girl so he can, in his words, "put my hand up her dress." Hip-hop star Usher enlists the help of Lil' Jon and Ludacris, in the song "Lovers and Friends," instructing a young woman "to be a good girl, turn around, and get these whippings, you know you like it like that." The music videos accompanying these songs are nothing more than soft porn brought to the world via MTV and BET—all the while sponsored by soft-drink giants like Coca Cola.

Music that animalizes sex, demeans women, and reduces men to Neanderthals should outrage women, but it does not. Surprisingly, young women comprise over 54percent of all urban music purchases. What an ironic twist—instead of boycotting the hip-hop industry, young women support the misogynist artists who degrade and humiliate them.

Female rappers share part of the blame. Female hipsters like Fantasia, in the chart topping song "Baby Mama," describes the hardships of single-parenthood but never says a word about taking sexual responsibility. Lil' Kim, in the song "Not Tonight," raps about the sexual domination of men. What would Lil' Kim say to Rosa Parks? "Mrs. Parks, thank you for your courage in the civil-rights struggle. Now black women have a chance to be devalued and sexualized by all Americans equally."

Rap music rules the airwaves in New York, Los Angeles, Chicago, San Francisco, Dallas, Philadelphia, Washington, D.C. and other major cities. Is it any wonder that sexism and racism "still" exist? With a diverse population of thirteen to thirty-four year old listeners from all backgrounds spending years digesting the lyrics of animalized thinking and behavior, what else would one expect?

Supply and demand conspire in this evil. Rappers degrade minority women, dehumanize themselves, and promote materialism; white suburban youth and women gobble it up; record companies have no scruples profiting from the arrangement.

Would Martin Luther King be proud of this? Is this why Harriet Tubman risked her life to lead slaves through the Underground Railroad? The current rap industry owes the civil-rights leaders of the 1950s and 1960s a huge apology. Middle-class suburbanites should be embarrassed.

The hip-hop generation gave rise to a multi-ethnic market of dehumanization that further erodes the fabric of civil society. Bad rap music will change its content only when Judeo-Christian values concerning God's design for human relationships, sex, and stewardship shape the minds and lives of both the producers and the consumers.

NEW LEADERSHIP NEEDED FOR KING'S OTHER DREAMS

Many Americans focus on Martin Luther King's "I Have A Dream" speech as if it were King's only address. Self-proclaimed "civil-rights leaders," dangle King's words before black communities like a well-worn fetish, a validation of their "anointed" political agenda. King's dreams, however, will become reality only if society rejects the ideas of those who have turned the black church into a political pawn. They must return instead, to the themes of the traditional black church that produced the civil-rights leaders of the past. King's later speeches reveal additional dreams for black Americans, dreams that leaders such as Jesse Jackson, Al Sharpton, Julian Bond, Maxine Waters, and many in the Congressional Black Caucus have failed to actualize.

The black church produced the likes of Rosa Parks, Martin King, Ralph Abernathy, Rev. Joseph E. Lowery, and others because of religious conviction and a burden for social justice and personal dignity. Its emphasis on social justice did not appear as a rationalization for a secular political agenda. Instead, it sprang from the moral imperatives derived from Scripture and the teaching of the Christian Church. The liberation narrative of Exodus carried special meaning for a people whose experience of the New World began in slavery. Black churches' defense of human dignity derived from their acceptance of the truth of man's creation in the image of God. The inherent moral dignity of the black individual is one central theme consistent from plantation churches to the black churches of the 1950s.

In this tradition, King, in his 1967 speech "Where Do We Go From Here," contended that, if America is to be great, blacks first "must massively assert our dignity and worth. We must stand up amidst a system that still oppresses us and develop an unassailable and majestic sense of values." The current "black leadership" conditions blacks to see themselves as perpetually inferior victims with no inherent dignity and no need of personal moral values.

Expecting the best of blacks is futile in this line of thinking. Young blacks hear throughout their entire lives that they are victims and that the world is set against them. Victimology accomplishes nothing but to undermine the higher goal of living as men and women of dignity. As a result, many blacks treat themselves, others, their families, and their communities as though they are without dignity, thereby fostering the nihilism reflected in broken families, drug abuse, violence, separatism, dependence, anti-intellectualism, and abortions. This is not what King had in mind.

He abhorred instilling a "false sense of inferiority" in blacks. However, young blacks learn that their so-called inferiority requires discriminatory programs to lower education standards for them. For example, high-school graduation requirements drop in predominantly minority school districts, and special programs exist, specifically designed to get "inferior" blacks admitted to college and graduate school.

King rejected this type of discrimination because it thrusts people into "idleness." Minority children, not called to greatness, therefore do not pursue it. Blacks, then, continue to be, in King's words, "branded as inferior or incompetent" by policies and programs that neither expect nor demand much of them.

King encouraged Americans to "be concerned that the potential of the individual is not wasted." However, this is exactly what occurred under the watch of the current leadership. The potential of individual blacks is wasted by herding them into sports and entertainment industries and schools with low standards, keeping blacks dependent on government programs, and shackling blacks to groupthink ideology. As King noted, "the dignity of the individual will flourish when the decisions concerning his life are in his own hands, when he has the means to seek self-improvement."

There is hope. There are black leaders who remain true to the themes of the black church and the vision of King's other dreams to call people to a lifestyle of great dignity. Among them are Bishop G.E. Patterson in Memphis, Rev. Lance Lewis in Philadelphia, Bishop Eddie Long in Atlanta, Bishop T.D. Jakes in Dallas, Rev. Weldon Williams in Chicago, and Bishop Charles E. Blake in Los Angeles. There are countless others. These pastors are calling blacks to lives of dignity in their sexuality, marriage, family, education, speech, personal morals, and business practices. If America is to be the great nation King dreamed of, it will take this new leadership to usher it to the next level.

PART FOUR

International

THE VIRTUOUS PATH TO AFRICAN DEVELOPMENT

A SOURCE OF GREAT frustration to those concerned with world poverty is the relative stagnation of much of the African continent. It is frustrating because widespread poverty is a function of human limitations, not the availability of natural resources. This fact renders less helpful the guidelines recently released under the title, Natural Resource Charter. Designed by an independent group of economists, lawyers and political scientists to help developing countries manage their natural resources to create real economic growth, the Charter provides helpful insights. Unfortunately, it inadequately emphasizes the crucial role of social mores beyond economics and political governance.

The African Development Bank (AfDB) Group's Chief Economist, Louis Kasekende, says that the Natural Resource Charter will help governments and societies rich in natural resources to manage such assets in a way that generates economic growth and promotes the people's welfare. Kasekende expressed these views on May 13 in Dakar, in reference to a presentation on the Natural Resource Charter during the AfDB's annual meeting.

Unlike many other development initiatives in Africa, the Resource Charter reminds one that additional actors are necessary for long-term sustainable growth, including "international companies, intergovernmental organizations, civil society groups, and the governments of resource-importing states." These "all have roles which affect the ability of societies to harness their endowments." Yet the focus rightly remains on "the governments of resource-rich countries themselves, since they have both the sovereign right, and the moral responsibility, to use the country's natural wealth for the benefit of their people."

The first principle of the Resource Charter is that "the development of natural resources should be designed to secure the maximum benefit for the citizens of the host country within the framework of its long-term development goals." The Charter provides eleven other precepts ranging from increased entrepreneurial competition to public spending priorities.

Even with a few questionable directives for government, the Charter is far superior to the economically naive Millennium Development Goals proffered by the World Bank and the United Nations, which contain no plans to create wealth in order to "end poverty." The Charter is also superior to the approach of the International Monetary Fund (IMF), which would also rather "reduce" poverty than create sustainable, wealth-generating economies in Africa. The IMF continues to operate under the misguided assumption that "greater progress toward meeting global poverty goals in Africa by 2015 will require further increases in government spending on critical public services."

What many of these organizations are beginning to understand is that many countries in Africa will escape poverty only if the African people elect quality leaders to positions of service. Entrepreneurial opportunities, the enforcement of property rights, the adjudication of conflicts, controlling violence, and terminating corruption are necessary aspects of an environment that will allow many African countries to develop out of poverty and remain vibrant. More importantly, to achieve success, these pillars of reform require the establishment of moral values. In the absence of virtue, the same system can serve to create new moral dilemmas. One must recognize the significant role of human limitations in structural reform.

For example, even though Nigeria is a democracy with many free-market principles, corruption rules the day and drags everyone else down with it. Halliburton, a U.S. construction firm, reputedly gave $180 million in bribes to top Nigerian politicians and government officials, including members of the Nigerian National Petroleum Corporation (NNPC), to win the contract for the construction of a liquefied natural gas plant.

In February, Halliburton agreed to pay $579 million to settle charges with the Securities and Exchange Commission and the Department of Justice over bribes KBR, a former Halliburton subsidiary, paid to win $6 billion in oil contracts from Nigerian officials. The bribe, in which three former Nigerian presidents were also said to have benefited, allegedly spanned the period from 1995, when the contract was awarded, to 2004 and possibly beyond. For successful change to occur, markets and governance must also value character and integrity.

The Natural Resource Charter could find a stronger voice on personal morality. Nevertheless, it is a definite step in the right direction, and one that many developing economies and international aid organizations should consider in the process of rethinking what is culturally and economically sustainable.

SAVING CHINA'S CHILDREN FROM THEIR GOVERNMENT

Heavy-handed government intervention without regard for human dignity produces long-term deleterious effects. Unintended consequences include a dehumanized social sphere and a debilitated economy. China's family planning policies, established nearly 30 years ago, are a case in point.

China's one-child policy, often enforced by coercive measures, has led to the systematic extermination of girls, a rise in child abductions, and a weakening of the Chinese family. It has created a market in human beings and decimated the traditional family-based system of old-age support. Immoral government mandates restricting the people's freedom to pursue the good bear evil fruit.

With most couples limited to one child, cultural and economic factors conspire to create a strong preference for male offspring. As a result, a market for boys has developed. Conservative estimates put the number of child abductions in China at 190 per day. Prices for stolen boys continue to rise, with levels approaching six months' of an average worker's wages. In 2006, 49-year-old Lin Yudi, was executed in southeastern China after she was found guilty of being part of a five-member gang involved in trafficking thirty-one baby boys. *The New York Times'* Andrew Jacobs reported on April 5 that the demand for baby boys is particularly strong in rural areas of South China. In the Fujian province, Su Qingcai, 38, recently spent $3,500 for a 5-year-old stolen boy.

Lower income parents find it difficult to get help from police to protect their children. Chinese authorities respond more faithfully to high profile cases of crimes affecting people with political connections.

It is another consequence of government-planned societies that elitism is enshrined; the police exist to protect the interests of the decision makers rather than the disempowered, regular citizen.

Article 240 of the Criminal Law of the People's Republic of China, adopted at the Second Session of the Fifth National People's Congress on July 1, 1979, made illegal the abducting, kidnapping, buying, trafficking in, fetching, sending, or transferring a woman or child, for the purpose of selling the victim. Unfortunately, these laws are not strictly enforced. Some Chinese activists attempted organizing private rescue groups to aid victimized children, but the central government is uncooperative with their efforts. The police have incentives to protect only the interests of the few.

The market for kidnapped boys, resulting from China's family planning policies, encourages sex-selective abortion of baby girls. In 2005, *The New England Journal of Medicine* reported that abortion after ultrasonography accounts for a large proportion of the decline in female birth rates. Estimates put the number of female sex-selected abortions at 40 million, generating a combination of one of the lowest fertility rates in the world and a disproportionately high number of male births.

Brides have thus become scarce. By 2000, among rural men, 27 percent at age 40 were unmarried. This situation has created demand for other illicit markets, resulting in the kidnapping and trafficking of women for marriage or the burgeoning sex industry, for example.

The shortage of children has also made the cost of care for the elderly an increasingly unbearable burden, according to Wang Feng, associate professor of sociology at the University of California, Irvine. As the elderly population balloons, approximately 70 percent of older Chinese depend on their children for vital financial support. Because married daughters usually shift their care allegiance to the husband's family, parents fear not having male heirs to care for them as they age. By 2025, using current fertility rates, Chinese 65 and older will constitute 25 percent of China's population. This dependent, elderly population will create an unsustainable burden on working adults and the government welfare system.

China's policy is another chapter in a long narrative of state intervention impinging on the freedom of the human individual. Government exists to protect and cultivate the family, which is vital for a flourishing social and economic order. Parents should be free to make virtuous decisions, consistent with the dignity of marriage, about their procreative contribution to society. China's policy uses the power of the state to violate parents' moral conscience. This coercion promotes abortion, fosters child trafficking, and puts the elderly at risk.

China's government should terminate all such policies. Permitting parents the freedom to pursue the goods of marriage is a basic requirement for a healthy civil society and long-term social and economic progress.

DEVELOPING NATIONS OFFER HOPE FOR U.S. RETAILERS

Even as economic forecasters predict a dark and cloudy market, one can spy a silver lining in the continued advance of globalization. As a new report on department stores indicates, the progress of developing economies promises to benefit the rest of the world as well—an outcome that comes as no surprise to those who understand international trade to be a win-win proposition.

The report, titled "Departmental Stores: A Global Outlook," by Global Industry Analysts Inc., shows developing nations emerging as centers of growth for department stores. "Booming economies, rising consumer affluence, changing purchasing patterns, and relatively lower levels of competition are driving departmental stores to benefit from the vast growth potential of the untapped markets," it says.

The new study highlights the fact that while developed countries offer limited growth opportunities because of market differentiation and competition, departmental stores are moving into developing nations such as India, China, Pakistan, Malaysia and Indonesia. Thanks to free-trade agreements and globalization, traditional American retailers are able to survive by offering new products and services in other countries.

This is good news for both developed and developing nations. Expanding international markets in the retail sector create jobs both in the United States and abroad.

For example, Toys "R" Us, with more than 680 stores in 33 countries outside of the United States, has successfully translated its business into foreign markets. The chain first entered the international scene in 1984 with stores in Canada and Singapore. In the first quarter of 2008, net international sales increased by $100 million, or 11 percent, to just over $1 billion, accounting for more than two-thirds of the company's growth.

That $1 billion in sales helps sustain the firm in the United States and enables it to provide improved products and services here and abroad.

This single example points to a simple but significant truth: globalization positions companies to remain vibrant here and throughout the world. In the States, Toys "R" Us faces an intensely competitive environment filled with strong companies like Target, Wal-Mart, and KB Toys, as well as other internet vendors. For the company to remain viable, it must move into new markets.

In developing countries, specialty retail stores and department stores introduce products, services, and jobs to people who previously had fewer choices. The wonder of international trade is that, even as companies pursue improvement in their bottom line, positive consequences accrue to all parties. Companies can grow and create opportunities while new beneficiaries gain access not only to the goods and employment generated directly, but also to those resulting from the ancillary business created by the interaction of local and international markets.

As department stores struggle with dynamic markets and changing demographics, there can be real local costs. When one hears news that the local department store is closing while new stores are opening oversees, it is important to remember that America's temporary loss is the gain of the world's economy (to which the U.S. belongs). The interim task is finding new opportunities for those who lose their jobs. Several partnerships between government, business, and the non-profit sectors have successfully transitioned these displaced workers into new jobs.

The mutually beneficial character of international exchange underscores the moral imperative for expanding free-trade agreements and encouraging companies to explore opportunities abroad. Doing so is the best strategy for helping the poor. Although greed and power lust drive some business leaders, one should not label the expansion of multinational companies "morally tainted." An alternative vision affirms multinational activity because it supplies the investment necessary for developing countries to create more wealth in their domestic economies.

Why would America not embrace increasing the standard of living for people in developing countries? Putting arbitrary limits on international trade through subsidies, tariffs, or measures intended to "stop shipping jobs oversees" actually weakens domestic businesses and perpetuates global poverty, especially among the world's truly disadvantaged people.

Global interdependence offers the best hope for lifting people out of poverty—it is a necessary part of maintaining a healthy, solvent global economy.

CHINA'S STEALTHY GLOBALIZATION

One of the pervasive myths of globalization critics, and G8 protestors, is the idea that the West alone is globalizing the world. This year's G8 summit outreach proved that China, in addition to being the world's greatest producer of greenhouse gases, is also stealthily globalizing the world. China's economic aggression in the Caribbean and Africa demonstrates two such examples of Asian globalization that may trump the West in years to come.

Leaders of the Group of Eight (G8) industrialized nations had two outreach sessions at this month's summit with five developing countries—Brazil, China, India, Mexico and South Africa—demonstrating that globalization is exactly that—global. This year's outreach marks the fourth time that Chinese President Hu Jintao attended the meeting as China's economy has grown at an impressive pace of more than 10 percent for five straight quarters with a GDP topping US$2.2 trillion in 2005, according to the World Bank.

In Jamaica, English and Chinese signs adorn many of the touring busses. This would seem odd until one discovers that China is investing millions in the Caribbean, especially in Jamaica. "Jamaica has become China's most important trade partner in the English-speaking Caribbean areas, "Chinese Premier Wen Jiabao said in 2005, adding that Jamaica's recognition of China's market economy has helped create favorable conditions for their bilateral economic and trade cooperation.

In May, Chinese Assistant Foreign Minister He Yafei hosted five Caribbean Community and Common Market (CARICOM) Caucus ambassadors in Beijing to encourage further diplomatic ties. Jamaica's Ambassador to China Wayne McCook, the coordinator of CARICOM Caucus of ambassadors, said they are ready to make substantive efforts with China to further cooperative ties with Caribbean countries.

The Chinese government reports that China-Jamaica trade volume in 2004 totaled $395.98 million, a 90.8 percent increase compared with the previous year. Chinese export volume accounted for $126.13 million, a 23.6 percent increase as compared with the previous year; and the Chinese import volume was $269.85 million, a 155.9 percent increase as compared with the previous year. China's major imports from Jamaica are cane sugar, aluminum and bauxite with primary exports in textiles, clothing and light industrial products.

China is also exerting its influence in Africa. The United Nations reports that China-African trade volume reached $56 billion in 2006. Chinese investors are active in 48 of the 53 African countries. The African Development Bank, which met in Shanghai in May, reported that Africa's economic growth rate reached 5.5 percent in 2006 and is expected to reach 5.9 percent and 5.7 percent in 2007 and 2008, respectively. The fast growth was mainly due to strong international demand for oil and mineral resources. Africa's growing agriculture sector will also contribute to future Asian investment.

The examples of the Caribbean and Africa point to an important dimension of China's economic expansion. Once a poor nation itself, China's prosperity, through trade, is now benefiting two of the most intractably underdeveloped regions of the world. As political activists and religious leaders in North America and Europe continue to call for more government-to-government aid in a well-intentioned but ineffective attempt to address poverty, China goes about ameliorating poverty by bringing the Caribbean and Africa into the global circle of exchange.

In 2007, Zambian President Levy Mwanawasa challenged the West to match Chinese investment in his country. Mwanawasa said Zambia welcomes Chinese investment, credit and loans, despite unease in the West over the fast pace of Chinese-African investment. "Those who oppose Chinese investment. . . .all they need to do is to equal the help we are getting from China. We only turned to the East when you people in the West let us down," Mwanawasa told Reuters on the sidelines of an African business forum. China has increased its planned investment to $900 million in the Zambia's mineral-rich Copper Belt industrial hub over the next four years.

Will Chinese culture swallow the indigenous African and Caribbean cultures? It is surprising that protestors remain mute on the subject of Chinese globalization. Perhaps, Americans and Europeans believe that the world's non-whites cannot develop economically. In the shortsighted, smug Western worldview, the West will always dominate global economy.

SPAIN'S AFRICAN IMMIGRANT PROBLEM

Spain's socialist government provided a nice red welcome mat for illegal African immigrants until March 11, 2004, when terrorists, most of whom came from Morocco, killed 190 people Immigration amnesty quickly became a security issue. Last month, the European Union's immigration chief announced plans to attract skilled African labor while boosting efforts to keep poor migrants out. Spain finds itself in a dilemma, simultaneously needing immigrants and seeking to curb them.

Spain's Canary Islands off West Africa, a popular European vacation spot, has become a favorite European entry point for Africans as well. This year alone nearly 24,000 people—about five times the number for all of 2005—were caught trying to reach the islands.

The new EU plan seeks to address shortages of skilled labor while stemming illegal immigration by offering $53 million to boost job creation in those African regions where most of the unskilled migrants to Europe originate. This strategy, however, will likely do little to solve the poverty, corruption, and violence that are at the source of African migration patterns.

The lack of electricity, jobs, education, and running water in many African regions creates desperation and a market for criminality, including human trafficking. Khalil Jemmah, a Moroccan aid worker, told FOX News that, "these people are so desperate they are ready to die . . . it's just a question of who gets here first, the smugglers or the terrorists." With only nine miles separating Africa from Europe, many desperate Africans attempt the dangerous journey to Spain in some of the world's most treacherous waters. The benefits of success outweigh the risks.

Spain's socialist government is stuck with the fact that the 700,000 immigrants granted amnesty last year live in a market structure that cannot absorb them. Ironically, Spain cannot afford to turn away large numbers of immigrants either. Because institutions like marriage and family seem irrelevant to many Spaniards, with the average woman bearing only 1.28 children in her lifetime, the scarcity of young workers cannot successfully support the socialist regime. Without immigrants, Spain may collapse. Josep Oliver, from Barcelona's Autonoma University told The Economist, "collectively we decided not to have children and, without knowing it, we decided to have immigrants."

Spain's service sector now dominates the economy, accounting for an estimated 66.5 percent of GDP in 2005. The thousands of low-skilled

African immigrants who fill these jobs rescued Spain from a social security crisis. In the service sector, retailing, tourism, banking and telecommunications contribute to critical economic growth, boosting the annual GDP to 3.7 percent. Spaniards need immigrants to meet their economy's demands. Spain, by some estimates, will need 4 million extra workers by 2020, a difficult quota to fill given the nation's casual attitude toward marriage and family.

Despite Spain's economic needs, the country must confront the desperate circumstances causing Africans to emigrate en mass—basic respect for human dignity requires this. Commitment to expanding the rule of law, property rights, and free markets will allow economic development in African nations, thus making any African migration to Europe a free choice instead of a desperate bid to escape from deadly poverty.

These problems are deeply rooted in European history.. Europe is paying the price for failing to champion African autonomy, liberty, and free economic development during the1884–1885 Berlin Conference, when colonial powers scrambled to gain control over the interior of the African continent. Decades later, the Cold War exacerbated the legacy of foreign intrusion and government coercion in Africa.

Europe should expect huge waves of immigrants as long as parts of Africa remain morally, politically, and economically unstable. Attractive European welfare benefits coupled with a dwindling European population also add to the problem. Moreover, as long as Spain and other nations rely on immigrants to fill the breach, the immigration movement will continue to grow. Africa's long-term political and economic problems are now Europe's problems as well, and $53 million is not enough to furnish the collateral benefits that would be the effect of African entrepreneurial societies ordered by law and liberty.

TOWARD FREEDOM IN THE ARAB WORLD

Regardless of one's view of the war in Iraq, one can agree on the desirability of a dignity-oriented freedom for individuals and families in the Arab world. Economic, political, and religious liberty, however, do not come in a valueless vacuum. Freedom rings in an ordered society, one in which all people, rich and poor alike, are free to pursue economic and moral goods. The same ordering that led to freedom in the Western world are the same ancient, time-tested truths that will bring liberty to all people everywhere in the world.

The Fraser Institute's recent report, titled "Freedom in the Arab World," points out that economic freedom in the Arab world is practicable only when individuals are free to acquire property without the use of force, fraud, or theft, and can freely use their property for the good. Additionally, sustained economic freedom in the Arab world will exist when individuals are free to use, exchange, or develop their property in ways that benefit them without violating the identical rights of others.

As history demonstrates, individuals or families who have the freedom to determine their own economic destiny find liberation from government dependence and long-term dependence on charity. This reminder is especially apt in developing economies all over the world. Positive changes in national economic growth rates rise only as both rich and poor alike enjoy equal structures for pursuing goods.

As the Fraser Institute's study indicates, many Arab states experienced economic growth in the past few years, but more work is necessary. For example, Lebanon, United Arab Emirates, and Yemen continue to lead the Arab world with low government expenditures, low taxes, and increased economic freedom for individuals, households, and businesses. Keeping the size of government small is a key mechanism in empowering those at the bottom. Tunisia and Morocco lead the Arab world in allowing people to exchange freely the fruits of their labor securely through the guarantees of property rights and rule of law.

Because of the oil industry, most Arab nations already possess stable currencies. Arab states have among the best records in the world in controlling inflation, though there is much room for improvement in Algeria, Libya, Morocco, and Syria. Oil states also have typically enjoyed freedom to trade internationally, as have both Lebanon and Jordan. However, reliance on oil revenue predictably has limited trade integration for the Arab states in other sectors, and there is much to be done to increase the prosperity of all citizens by promoting international trade of non-oil related products.

Governmental regulatory restraints and red tape will destroy new businesses and retard job creation unless the ever-increasing regulatory burdens are thwarted. The Gulf States have successfully managed to stave off much governmental regulatory interference, unlike Western Europe and the United States. Other Arab states, though, including Egypt, Syria,

Algeria, and Mauritania, remain some of the most interfered-with economies in the Arab world and it shows.

Many forget that the Bush Administration spent considerable time consulting with many Arab states to increase economic freedom for all— rich and poor, men and women. The Middle East Partnership Initiative (MEPI) established by then-Secretary of State Colin Powell in 2002, created grassroots educational opportunities, promoted economic liberty and private sector development, and strengthened civil society and the rule of law throughout the region. The initiative provided a framework and funding for the United States to expand the four pillars of MEPI: economics, politics, education, and women's empowerment.

An ordered liberty, grounded in the transcendent equality of the human person, is an ancient ideal rooted in the era of Moses and the Torah. Protection of property, exploration of vocation, charity and surplus for the needy, fair and just treatment of immigrants and employees, free exchange of goods, enforceable contracts, and the like are not "western" ideas. They are, in fact, eastern principles that originated from the very region now needing to recover these expressions of human freedom first articulated thousands of years ago.

GLOBAL GOODS FOR THE ANTI-GLOBALIZATION MOVEMENT

An anti-globalization group called "Anti-Marketing" defines globalization as "the process of exploiting economically weak countries by connecting the economies of the world, forcing dependence on (and ultimately servitude to) the western capitalist machine." While this formulation may sound extreme, the same basic, perverted understanding of globalization has poisoned the minds of many.

In a world of scarcity, the most advanced societies have the most internationally connected economies. This has always been true. In ancient northern African nations, the Greco-Roman world, and later in the Netherlands, Britain, Spain, and the United States, nations that traded widely were nations that prospered.

Trading societies also tend to be open societies. The Scriptures expose the proclivity of people in any system to be "lovers of themselves, lovers of money, boastful, arrogant, abusive . . ." (2 Tim 3:2–3). However, the assumption that societies isolated from the world promote human dignity and increase human freedom better than internationally connected ones proves historically false. Isolationist nations lag behind the rest of the world in terms of both human freedom and standards of living. It is no accident that the developed nations of the West offer more freedom and protection for women and non-elite citizens. Connecting weak economies to stronger ones, overall, is mutually beneficial and empowers developing countries toward true independence for its citizenry.

This is exactly what happened when the Japanese economy joined the global market. Japan's isolation from the West rendered it technologically and economically weedy. After opening trade with the West in 1854, Japanese leaders and scholars of the Meiji era studied the United States and its key formative figures like Abraham Lincoln and Benjamin Franklin. In the span of three generations, Japan grew from an isolated, agrarian economy, to the second largest economy in the world—on an island with relatively few natural resources.

Within the context of global trade, Japanese innovators took Western products and made them their own—actually improving them to sell back to the world cheaper and better than originally produced. By 1958, just over a hundred years after opening trade with the West, America's first Nissan dealership opened for business in San Diego, offering the $1,695 PL210 four-door Datsun sedan. The dealership sold only 83 vehicles. At the time, analysts believed that Japanese automakers would never be major players in the U.S. market.

By the late 1980s, Japanese cars accounted for more than 30 percent of the U.S. market. The island nation continues to lead the world in technological advancement in electronics, robotics, and transportation. Japan became the second largest economy in the world by connecting its economy with the rest of the world.

The irony of the anti-globalization movement, that the protestors themselves rely on and benefit from globalization, means that they are biting the hand that feeds them. Western protesters use their freedom and wealth to buy Nokia cell phones and Seiko digital watches. They drive their Subaru Outbacks, plastered with bumper stickers, to protest rallies. There, they use Canon digital cameras (or Nikon 35mm cameras with Fuji film) to snap photos for millions of people to view on the Internet or on televisions made by Sony or Toshiba.

In fact, much of the anti-globalization angst is nothing but old school paternalism cloaked in concern for other cultures. The protesters presume that only Westerners have the economic savvy to request, receive, and handle imported products. For example, a Guatemalan franchise like Pollo Campero Fried Chicken is good for Los Angeles, but GAP clothes and Coca-Cola are destructive to other countries. Saabs, Volkswagens, Volvos and other foreign products benefit only those sophisticated enough to purchase them without undermining fragile native cultures. North Americans and Europeans comfortably surround themselves with imported accoutrements, while the benighted developing world remains shackled to the enslavement of Western foreign aid programs.

In the process of connecting economies, exports may include filth and evil, a fact that highlights the need for a sound moral culture without which political and economic structures function ineffectively and harmfully. This is where globalization worry should focus. Meanwhile, the misguided complain about MTV throughout the world but say nothing about Reggaeton, the latest Latin music craze, polluting the airwaves all over the United States and Latin America. The real enemy is not connecting economies of prosperity but connecting economies of evil.

THE CHAVEZ ROAD TO SERFDOM

Liberty and democracy in Venezuela are crumbling under the dictatorial leadership of Hugo Chavez. Venezuela, the world's fifth largest oil exporter, has an unemployment rate nearing 21 percent. The government monopolizes and mismanages the country's most valuable natural resource, with its potential yearly earnings of $130 billion dollars. Under the Castro-style leadership of Hugo Chavez, the rule of law and promotion of property rights is nothing more than a fairy tale. To date, more than 3 million citizens, aware of these facts, have formally demonstrated their desire to have Chavez removed immediately, before the nation collapses.

These 3 million people signed a petition calling for a recall referendum on the despotic rule of Chavez. The five-member National Electoral Council, unfortunately, recently rejected this petition. Venezuela's Constitution allows a petition for a recall halfway through a president's term of six years. The council voted 3–0, with two abstentions, to reject the petition because the signatures were collected too many months before the August 19 halfway point of Chavez's current six-year reign, which began in 2000. The petition effort to recall Chavez, as a result, will resume in October.

The recall effort has won the full support of the Catholic bishops' conference of Venezuela. Archbishop Baltazar Enrique Porras Cardozo of Merida, citing the "great insults committed by the president of the nation, Hugo Chavez," called for the urgent holding of the recall referendum, as provided in the nation's Constitution.

Chavez, a former military officer, was involved in a failed 1992 coup to overthrow the government of President Carlos Andres Perez. Chavez spent two years in prison before bursting onto the political scene a few years later in 1998, declaring Marxist class warfare in Venezuela and winning the presidency. He promised to use the coercive power of the state to bridge the gap between the wealthy and the poor. However, under his reign, poverty has actually increased. In addition, corruption and violence are now the norm. There have been several national strikes crippling the oil industry, the economy is in decline, and the national currency, the Bolivar, plummeted 25 percent against the dollar last year as the government instituted exchange rate controls. This explains why his approval rating hovers at 35 percent.

President Chavez, who expressed admiration for Fidel Castro, recently instituted new policies and programs in the wake of the recall petition. The *L.A. Times* reports that Chavez now provides basic reading and writing instruction for the poor. Hundreds of thousands of children attend school for the first time. Government credits give poor families the ability to plant crops, organize businesses, repair homes, and so on. Last week, Chavez's personal attempt to teach literacy classes to poor children via a live, two-hour broadcast from his palace fell flat when he misspelled a simple verb. The government interrupted all other television programming to broadcast the event. (Venezuelan telecommunication laws grant the president the power to break into television broadcasts at his whim.)

Any astute observer of these antics can see that this president's recent post-petition reforms are a public relations ruse designed to maintain political control. As a champion of Cuban-style communism and a friend of the deposed Saddam Hussein and his regime, Chavez is merely dangling a carrot in front of the poor, promising to use force to bring down those who produce the nation's wealth. He refers to business owners as "fascists." While it is true that many in the Venezuelan business community routinely produce inferior goods and provide substandard work environments, turning free enterprise into the enemy has led to economic disaster.

The government issued credits to the poor for the purchase of homes, but those who participate can sell their homes only in the case of an emergency and with government permission. The poor, duped into believing that they have property rights, will ultimately realize that the government has the final authority on how the land is used. The poor still enjoy no economic liberty, even though the government would like them to think otherwise.

A new state sponsored television network will soon begin broadcasting operations, organized by Chavez in response to the privately owned Venezuelan media's anti-government programming In other words, the private stations promote free speech and air the opinions of the citizens. The government can support and promote its own best interests on state television. In some countries, like Castro's Cuba or the Iraq of Sadam Hussein, people might call this new station a propaganda machine and a tool to distract the masses from the real issues that plague the nation: namely, the political and economic enslavement of Venezuelans.

What remains absent from much analysis on Venezuela is specifying which political and economic structures promote human dignity and freedom. Chavez is correct to promote home ownership, but poor Venezuelans should have plenary ownership, granting them freedom to use the land in ways that best meet the needs of individual families and communities. Moreover, there is no effective check on the power of Chavez and his government. The political apathy of the business sector effectively cripples the entire nation's economic prosperity. The Venezuelan Constitution, ratified by its citizens—not the opinions of Chavez's inner circle—must form the basis of law. Poverty fosters illiteracy, increasing the poor's dependence on surrogates for sustenance and knowledge. As a result, Venezuelans do not control their own political and economic future.

If Chavez were a real champion of the people, he would improve the living conditions of all Venezuelans, leading them to lives of independence rather than subjugation. Complete privatization of the oil industry would be a great first step, leading to the development of ancillary markets, increasing employment opportunities, and thereby bolstering the wealth of the poor. Without free enterprise and the decentralization of power, Venezuela will never actualize its $130 billion potential. In the final analysis, the primary obstacle to economic and political liberty in Venezuela is the government of Hugo Chavez—an opinion shared by more than 3 million Venezuelans.

GUATEMALA AT THE CROSSROADS: THE FUTURE OF FREE MARKET REFORMS

Interest in building a free and virtuous society thrives in Central America, as evidenced by a series of March conferences held in Guatemala City, Guatemala. These conferences brought together some of the nation's most prominent religious, business, and political leaders. The conferences, organized by the Instituto para la Productividad con Responsibilidad (IPRES), the Instituto de Gobernanza, and El Shaddai Church, were designed to deal with a host of issues critical to the future of Guatemala's social and economic development. The rule of law, social contract, private property, limited government, the social responsibility of the church, private charity, and vocation are just a few examples of the topics covered. The mere fact that these events garnered such a diverse audience of participants, of differing religious traditions and professional backgrounds, indicates the widespread desire to free the wealth-generating potential of the market within a supportive moral culture.

Guatemala, a nation with a gross domestic product (GDP) of around $20 billion, is still recovering from a brutal 36-year civil war—a war that ended less than a decade ago. While the country is rich in natural resources, real GDP growth has been sluggish over the past several years, averaging around 3 percent annually. In 1998, GDP growth in Guatemala was 5.2 percent, up from 3.1 in 1996. By the end of 2002, estimated GDP growth was only about 2 percent. Currently, corruption in the national government is the norm, drug trafficking flourishes throughout the country, and poverty is widespread. As the largest economy in Central America, the economic and political situation of Guatemala affects the entire region.

Prior to the country's present administration, Guatemala underwent significant economic and political development. Under the leadership of President Alfonso Portillo, however, the country experienced a sharp reversal of many of the pre-1999 free-market reforms. The Portillo Administration's enactment of higher taxes and its cavalier treatment of the rule of law have stymied the nation's economic development.

These conditions brought about a renewed interest in the free-market reforms that characterized government policy in the 1990s. The March conferences, designed to bring together some of Guatemala's "best and brightest," discussed the future of free market reforms and, by extension, the very future of Guatemala itself. The fundamental conviction of all the sponsoring organizations is that Guatemala's future lies not with a centralized federal structure dictating economic policy, but with the economic and moral components of a revitalized civil society working in concert for the economic development of Guatemala.

Rodrigo Callejas, an attorney from Guatemala City and one of the conference organizers, provides critical insight into the changes necessary to unlock the economic and political potential of Guatemala. Callejas notes that, to ensure Guatemala's continued economic growth, "a national dialogue has to be set in order for all sectors of Guatemalan society to agree upon a long-term national vision, based upon a stable legal framework, rule of law, a democratic government, and a socially-aware free market economic system."

However, like other countries in the region, an unwieldy, overbearing federal structure blocks the desired free-market "culture" needed for long-term, systemic change in Guatemala. This structure makes Guatemala, especially as perceived by many investors, a very unfriendly place to do business. Significant structural reforms are needed—and needed immediately—if Guatemala is to survive and compete in the international marketplace. Callejas is convinced that new growth will ensue when Guatemala capitalizes its assets and when there is "a single tributary scheme that will motivate investors and provide them with the stability for their investments."

Perhaps such a possibility looms more imminently than one imagines, since federal elections are scheduled for November. The next generation of Guatemala's leaders, like Callejas, wants to improve economic conditions by seeking "to take away the overwhelming power that the government actually has, and decentralize it to the civil society." Guatemala needs a new vision, continues Callejas, one in which "the government has to understand that its role is to serve. . . and respond to the needs of entrepreneurs in a just and efficient way."

His is not a lone voice. Organizations such as IPRES explore and disseminate the dynamic relationship between ethics, social responsibility, and the institutions of the free-market. A fundamental principle of The Instituto de Gobernanza is to promote the principles of limited government and respect for the autonomy of civil society.

What is going on in Guatemala? There is a sense among this new generation of leaders that the country is poised on the verge of unprecedented social and economic gains. Free-market principles set in their proper moral framework provide these leaders and institutions with the hope that Guatemala will be a model society in Latin America—a society that provides moral, social, and economic opportunities for all its citizens.

Because of the seemingly intractable nature of the aforementioned issues, the next election will prove to be one of the most important in the nation's history. Until the drug trafficking network collapses, however, the overall safety of Guatemalan society remains a significant concern. The next administration must simply reconfigure the outrageous tax policy that stifles entrepreneurs and suffocates the economy. Rampant government corruption must be addressed and successfully prosecuted. The next president must take the long view of political and economic reform, focusing on those reforms necessary to obtaining the long-term benefits of a free market system, set within the appropriate moral framework. One should hope and pray that the next generation of Guatemala's leaders remains committed to pursuing a society that is both free and virtuous, for the sake of the country and the good of Central America.

THE LAWLESS LEADERSHIP OF ZIMBABWE

As the situation in the African nation of Zimbabwe continues to worsen under the corrupt regime of Robert Mugabe, one must ascertain how this once prosperous "bread basket" of Africa is now home to millions of starving people. A brief examination of the lawless tradition of leadership in this troubled nation gives some clue as to how the country has degenerated into its present madness. Such an examination offers clear evidence that economic prosperity is sustainable only when the government fairly and equitably applies the rule of law and the preservation of human dignity serves as the foundation of just governance.

Tragically, the history of Zimbabwe illustrates the destructive legacy of an exploitative colonialism. The colonialism experienced by Zimbabwe placed colonial interests over the needs of indigenous people. Thus, from the beginning, human dignity was diminished and property rights ignored, at least for those not in the ruling elite. The occupying

British in no way applied the rule of law impartially to all people of Zimbabwe. British colonial power governed Zimbabwe in an autocratic fashion, inaugurating a tradition of autocratic rule. This tradition of autocratic rule allowed leaders to pursue their own interests, rather than those of the nation, leading to endemic instability and aggression. In this regard, Robert Mugabe has learned the lessons of his predecessors well.

Some History

In 1889, the British Crown granted Cecil Rhodes a charter to establish a mining company giving him the authority to settle the vast area currently called Zimbabwe. After obtaining a concession for mineral rights from the local tribal chiefs, he began a wide-ranging land grab. In 1893, the colonialists attacked and defeated the Ndebele kingdom. Confiscated land and livestock became the property of the white settlers, a story not unlike that of the Native Americans.

In a display of hubris, Cecil Rhodes named his newly conquered territory "Rhodesia." With wide swaths of fertile land and a region rich with natural resources under his control, Rhodes set about making Rhodesia a place of prosperity. By using advanced agricultural techniques and innovative mining technologies from the West, it was not long before colonial settlers enjoyed high levels of wealth.

In 1930, the ruling elite passed the Land Apportionment Act. This act gave the white minority (5 per cent of the population) over fifty percent of the conquered land of Rhodesia. Partially because of this development, indigenous political resistance to colonial rule began to take form and shape. Tensions would continue to rise for decades.

In 1965, Ian Douglas Smith declared Rhodesia's independence from Britain. The British government wanted eventual indigenous rule in Rhodesia but the ruling elite resisted any power sharing. The United Nations levied sanctions against the nation but Smith simply ignored international consensus on the matter and continued with his own plan, another all too familiar scenario in history.

The Land Reform Politics of Robert Mugabe

Britain simply turned its head; meanwhile the Zimbabwe African People's Union (ZAPU) and the Zimbabwe African National Union (ZANU) organized anti-government political movements directed at restoring a majority rule. During the 1970s, a bloodbath began when the indigenous majority sought to regain control of the land. The violence was unprecedented and, in 1980, British and American negotiators developed the Lancaster House Agreement aimed at implementing majority rule and the rule of law. As a result, Robert Mugabe was installed as prime minister

After Mugabe's installation, Rhodesia became Zimbabwe. An ad hoc land reform program proposed the passing of property from the white settlers to indigenous citizens, as the transfer of power segued into majority rule The ZANU and ZAPU organizations combined forces securing Mugabe's re-election to the presidency in 1996.

In 1997, Mugabe, in the autocratic tradition of the country, announced a new land reform program redistributing farmland, by force if necessary, to non-white Zimbabweans. The international community was outraged at these actions so Mugabe's government did not press the issue. The issue, however, remained important in domestic political calculations, as it was painfully obvious that nearly 70 percent of the best farmland belonged to 5 per cent of the population. The political opportunity to consolidate power was too great to ignore.

The white minority lost its political hegemony by relinquishing all government control to Mugabe and his associates. Within Mugabe's regime there has been much recent infighting between former rival political factions dating from the political conflicts of the seventies and eighties. This infighting created uncertainty for Mugabe's political future and the land reform program served as a prime opportunity for Mugabe to reassert himself. Mugabe, acting solely in his own political self-interest, obviously cares little about the welfare of his nation. Hundreds of thousands of his own people are expected to die from the twin plagues of AIDS and politically contrived starvation. Mugabe and his cronies are securing their own future under the guise of seeking what is best for the nation as whole.

A Lawless Nation

The difficulty with analyzing the Zimbabwe situation through the lens of Western political values is that Zimbabwe, despite its rule by a Western power, has never been governed by the best principles of Western governance. Beginning in the 1890s, Zimbabwe has been ruled in an autocratic fashion. The country never developed a system of property rights and protection because neither Rhodes nor Smith governed in a way consistent with these principles. Rhodes granted some mineral rights concessions, but then simply took the rest of the land for the colonial settlers. Smith snubbed his nose at British insistence that Africans have political rights.

The rule of law, in any form, has been absent throughout the entire history of Zimbabwe, in part because the nation never operated under the assumption that such a rule had any value. Under colonial rule, the rule of law applied only to white settlers. The rule of law was exercised only as it accelerated Rhodes' conquest of the land. This also explains why Smith abandoned rule of law as it applied to his diminished role as leader and rejected the British government's demand to construct a plan to return rule to the demographic majority.

Mugabe, continuing in the tradition established by his predecessors, is ignoring numerous legitimate trans-national and international authorities and securing absolute political rule for himself. To seal his consolidation of power, last Friday, Mugabe dissolved his cabinet and replaced them with his pliable cronies. The oppressed has now become the oppressor. Mugabe seized power in the same fashion and by using the same strategies as the colonial elites he so derides.

The autocratic and despotic cycle of leadership cannot continue if people are truly concerned about the sanctity of human life and welfare of the people of Zimbabwe. Mugabe denies the Zimbabweans the basic freedoms that would allow them to feed their families and stabilize the nation. The tyrannical mismanagement of Zimbabwe opened the door to famine and disease, devastating a once vital nation with enormous potential.

Zimbabwe needs sweeping constitutional reform and economic restructuring. Racial and economic reconciliation using methods proven successful in South Africa may be effective in Zimbabwe, as well. The cycle of political chaos perpetuated by the elites, white or black, must end. In this regard, the African nations must establish and support a climate conducive to peace, political stability, and economic vitality. Unfortunately, efforts by neighboring countries to rein in Mugabe's rule have yet to materialize.

Currently, the moral and cultural context necessary to institutionalize principles of national reform, such as rule of law based in the preservation of human dignity, property rights, individual liberty, free-market initiatives, entrepreneurship, improved education, and quality healthcare simply do not exist. These are just a few of the many ingredients needed to develop a properly functioning national life and the vibrant civil society necessary to hold it together.

To understand Zimbabwe's current state of affairs, one must understand the historical context that fomented Zimbabwe's problems. Nevertheless, while self-interested autocratic rule in Zimbabwe continues, chaos will also rule and people will continue to die. As international attention focuses on Zimbabwe's dire situation, there is some hope for reform. It is important to note, however, that in Zimbabwean politics, "past is prologue."

PART FIVE

Education

PUBLIC SCHOOLS FLUNK THE TEST ON BLACK MALES

D O AT-RISK BLACK MALES need to be emancipated en masse from American public schools? A newly released study regarding high school dropout and incarceration rates among blacks raises the question. Nearly 23 percent of all black American male high school dropouts, ages sixteen to twenty-four, are in jail, prison, or a juvenile justice institution, according to "Consequences of Dropping Out of High School," published by Northeastern University's Center for Labor Markets.

High school dropouts cost the nation dearly. Not only are American taxpayers receiving no return on the $8,701 spent on average per student, each dropout costs $292,000 over his lifetime in lost earnings, lower taxes paid, and higher spending for social programs like incarceration, health care, and welfare.

Given the many social pathologies plaguing black males in low-income and fatherless households, is the failed public school paradigm the best solution for at-risk black males? Since public schools, by law, cannot teach virtue and often reduce children to receptacles of information, expanding private and faith-based options to black parents is the only compelling solution.

The Office for Standards in Education, Children's Services and Skills (Ofsted), England's chief education inspection agency, recently released a report lauding the attributes of faith schools. The report, "Independent Faith Schools," examined the quality of moral development taught by Christian, Jewish, Muslim, Buddhist and Hindu religious schools. The inspectors found "pupils demonstrating an excellent understanding of spiritual and moral attributes." In all the schools visited, "pupils gained a strong sense of identity and of belonging to their faith, their school and to Britain." In other words, faith-based schools, simply by teaching religion and values, develop moral standards in their students. Embracing religious beliefs leads students to become virtuous citizens, citizens capable of making good life choices.

Has America surrendered the job of making virtuous citizens out of black males? In England's faith schools, "good citizenship was considered by all the schools visited to be the duty of a good believer because this honoured the faith," the report says. In contrast, American public schools serve as prisoner factories for at-risk black males. Because producing educated, virtuous citizens is unrelated to funding, throwing money at the problem fails to address the true issues. The simplistic expedient of increasing government allocations to education changes nothing. Moreover, until the American education system follows the lead of faith-based British schools, nothing will change. English faith-based schools produce students with good "spiritual, moral, social and cultural understanding." America can and should do likewise.

Even in the public sector, blacks realize that the current model fails black males. Kentucky State University President Mary Sias says the university is seeking funding to open a boarding school for black male youth to prepare them for college. The Eagle Academy for Young Men, a charter school in the Bronx, is the first all-male public school in New York City in 30 years. Eagle Academy has a high school graduation rate of 82 percent, compared with approximately 51.4 percent of black and 48.7 percent of Hispanic students graduating from high schools citywide. This may explain why Eagle Academy had 1,200 applications for this year's ninth-grade class of eighty students.

Why do the education elites want to keep at-risk black males in schools that dump them in the streets or jail? Why is America content with the lie that funding is the problem? The District of Columbia spends $12,979 per student and has a black male graduation rate of 55 percent, compared to 84 percent for whites. Illinois spends over $8,000 per students with a black male graduation rate of 41 percent, compared to 82 percent for whites. When will the American government emancipate black parents and stop telling them what to do with their children?

Americans cannot afford, financially or morally, to culture black male criminality in the Petri dishes America calls public schools. Even though charter schools, vouchers, and tax-credit programs reflect some progress, black parents need radical new options that empower them with absolute freedom to choose the best schools. While every at-risk black male does not have access to good faith-based opportunities, the only hope for liberating young black males to actualize their potential to be productive participants in a global economy and virtuous citizens of a healthy nation is to free black parents from the tyranny of government bureaucrats. Black America needs a "Freedom of Choice" movement.

HIGH SCHOOL HIV SCARE POINTS TO MORAL CRISIS

All over the world, news agencies are reporting the startling revelation that Normandy High School students in suburban St. Louis, Missouri must be tested for HIV after an infected person told health officials that as many as fifty teenagers might have been exposed to the AIDS virus. While public officials are calling for more education, the root of the problem is profoundly moral and cultural.

School administrators did not release any details describing how the virus may have spread in the school. However, the usual suspects, drug use and sexual activity, must play a role. This is yet another item on a list of problems plaguing a district already known to be among the worst academically performing districts in Missouri and in jeopardy of losing its accreditation.

If the virus entered the high school because of sexual activity, this story serves as a cautionary tale about adolescent sexual morality. According to the most recent date from the Centers for Disease Control, nearly 48 percent of high school students report having sex. Even worse, some 15 percent of high school students report having four or more partners.

Because Normandy High School's student body is nearly 99 percent black, the stereotyped analysis of the neighborhood's demographics lead people to say, "We are not surprised." In other words, "there go those blacks living the sexual lives displayed in hip hop." Beyond the racially charged stereotypes, however, this potential tragedy confirms the existence of widespread sexual confusion among teenagers in general.

In 1996, the PBS documentary, "The Lost Children of Rockdale County," recounted a syphilis outbreak in an upper-middle class, predominantly white Atlanta suburb that affected more than 200 teenagers. The documentary revealed secret aspects of these teenagers' lives, such as group sex, binge drinking, drugs and violence. Not surprisingly, their parents had no clue about what was going on. Some of the students involved in the epidemic were as young as twelve years of age.

In a culture that glamorizes and celebrates non-marital, extra-marital, impulse-driven sexuality it is no wonder children are confused about the purpose of their sexuality. Ill-equipped and cowardly parents relinquish the duty of sex education to teachers or the federal government. Additionally, religious leaders often fail in their responsibility to assist parents in nurturing their children's sexual lives by teaching them about God's plan for his people—to live a sexual life characterized by fidelity and virtue.

As a result, high school students resort to learning about sex primarily from movies, music, internet pornography, and television programs—or, even worse, their parents' own sexual infidelities.

Many high school boys stoop to using girls' bodies as tools in some sort of right-of-passage ritual affirming their masculinity. Many high school girls worry more about getting pregnant than they do about contracting STDs and HIV. These children are sexually desensitized; their risky behavior, therefore, carries no consequences.

Preserving sex for the context of life-long, committed love has disappeared along with the wisdom of delayed gratification. As the Rev. E. Dewey Smith, Jr. reminds teenagers, "You have the rest of your lives to have sex."

Does America harbor lower expectations of its people than of its animals? Dogs cannot control themselves, so their owners spay and neuter them. People, on the other hand, have choices. They choose to either indulge or curb their impulses and desires. "Raging hormones" do not overwhelm reason and virtue. Biology is no excuse for low expectations. High school students can preserve sex for life-long, committed love because they are human beings.

If America's children contract STDs and HIV, this will profoundly affect society as a whole, including the American economy. Expenditures for STD treatment strain an already troubled health system. A sick and dying workforce saps economic vitality. Engaging in behavior that is physically and morally debilitating in no way prepares one to participate in a competitive global economy.

Dehumanizing sexuality sabotages personal identity, the family, and the public good. Like Rockdale county, perhaps Normandy High School is another wake-up call to baby-boomers that their sexual revolution is damaging—in some cases killing—their children and grandchildren.

BETTER GRADES THROUGH BLING-BLING

With alarming failure rates at the nation's inner city schools, one wants to celebrate any attempt to motivate success. Still, one must examine the motivation and its likely or demonstrated results. A new concept gaining attention suggests that children earn immediate cash or gift rewards for completing normal academic tasks, such as homework. While such programs are well intentioned, hustling minority kids with"bling-bling" is sure to cultivate materialism and deteriorate family relationships.

Harvard economist Roland Fryer developed the Sparks Incentive program in an effort to raise achievement scores for America's black children. In the pay-to-learn scheme, children never discover the joys of mastering a subject or of finding intrinsic meaning in their studies. They focus, instead, on earning money rather than the intangible rewards of scholastic excellence. Seduced into pursuing the vanity of money, children fail to learn the lesson of delayed gratification. One of the most important principles of long-term success in anything is totally incapacitated.

Last year, the New York City schools, desperate for solutions, hired Fryer as its Chief Equality Officer. His job was to figure out how to narrow the racial gap in achievement in the city's schools. Today, over 5,000 students in the New York City public school system are participating in this privately funded program. In one Brooklyn elementary school, students can earn up to $250 a year. School districts in at least twelve states have similar incentive programs, including the cities of Atlanta, Dallas, and Baltimore.

One misguided school even offers free cell phones as an incentive. Fryer defends this rueful practice saying, "[with] cell phones, [as] financial rewards for kids, we're meeting kids where they are and giving them rewards to do the things that we want them to do," What comes next? Free sagging pants? Coupons for weaves, rims, designer jeans, gold chains, and gold-teeth grills?

This type of disregard for the practical effects produced by striving for good ends via dubious means reduces the humanity of entire families. Black kids are more than simply a variable in a complex economic algorithm applied to education philosophy. Black kids are human beings with inherent dignity. They need direction to grow into virtuous adults who contribute positively to the world within the context of family and community.

Clinical psychologist Dr. Madeline Levine, author of *The Price of Privilege*, refutes paying cash for grades, condemning the practice as a psychologically damaging approach to education. Manipulating behavior with financial incentives profoundly sabotages the internal mechanisms needed to form the character and integrity required for adulthood.

Hustling performance with cash can never substitute, Levine argues, "for parental interest, presence, and guidance." It leads to a lessening of parental influence and cultivates greed. One would think that America's public school system would not wish to cultivate "bling, bling" ideology.

Children have a nascent ability to desire and appreciate parental approval. Once upon a time, schools challenged children to perform well—or else parents would be involved. Children knowing, early on, that they are accountable to their parents—and that other adults cooperate in that accountability—creates conditions for healthy family life in general.

The late Professor Randy Pausch of Carnegie Mellon University railed against the deification of material goods as incentives for living well at the school's commencement ceremony on May 18, 2008. Pausch encouraged graduates to pursue meaningful vocations that stirred their spirits. "You will not find that passion in things," he warned, "and you will not find that passion in money."

When asked if paying cash for performance might send a message to children that learning is not its own reward, Fryer responded, "Those are not my concerns. My biggest concern is [that] we don't do anything." Why is cultivating self-centered materialism and breaking down parent/child relationships the only alternative to doing nothing? Herein rests the problem of hiring an economist who may not have the wherewithal to connect economics to the formation of children with character and integrity.

While economics teaches helpful things about the role of incentives, the dignity of children and the integrity of family life cannot be subverted for algorithmic results. Ignoring the character process will produce a generation of children who can perform on exams but have little humanity.

ONE MILLION REASONS
FOR RADICAL EDUCATION REFORM

More than 1.23 million high school seniors will fail to graduate in the class of 2008, according to a new study conducted by the Editorial Projects in Education (EPE) Research Center. Now that the drama over the Democratic nominee has subsided, the presidential candidates must return to issues that threaten to hobble America in a global economy: namely, millions of future adults who are not acquiring the skill sets that will enable them to compete.

Results for the class of 2005, the most recent year available, show a national graduation rate of nearly 71 percent, an increase of about half a percentage point over the prior year. According to the report, that figure drops for historically disadvantaged groups: 58 percent for Hispanics, 55 percent for African-Americans, and 51 percent for Native Americans. Males in these groups fare especially poorly.

Iowa, New Jersey, Pennsylvania, Wisconsin, and Vermont lead the nation with graduation rates of more than 80 percent. The District of Columbia, Georgia, Louisiana, Nevada, New Mexico, and South Carolina lag the nation with rates under 60 percent.

The new data are highlighted in a report, "Diplomas Count 2008: School to College: Can State P-16 Councils Ease the Transition?", which explores the graduation crisis for every U.S. district and state. "The nation and many states face severe challenges in graduating students from high school. The crisis disproportionately strikes poor, minority, and urban youths. With the graduation rate rising less than one percentage point annually in recent years, we still have much work to do," says Christopher Swanson, Director of the EPE Research Center.

What reports overlook, and all the political rhetoric during presidential campaigns miss, is that high school graduation rates reflect a stable family life, a sense of self-efficacy, and moral agency, rather than the amount of money spent per pupil or the number of standardized assessments administered from kindergarten through grade twelve.

Fatherless children are twice as likely to drop out of school as their classmates who live with two parents. Children with absentee fathers consistently score lower than the norm in reading and math tests.

High school teachers notice a trend year after year: students from the most stable families and loving communities usually were the most successful. Some of the brightest students are not free to perform well because of chaos at home. Children from abusive homes and children of divorced or absentee parents did not normally perform well regardless of aptitude. Some students who regularly receive low marks often score high on aptitude and IQ tests.

Self-efficacy grows when a child believes that his or her life has meaning and that he or she can make a difference in the world. What better incentive to learn about the world and learn a skill set than the knowledge that someday one will contribute to making the world a better place? Materialism and consumption as motivators eventually fail to provide incentives for struggling children to persevere. A high school student who is depressed, abusing drugs, suicidal, and nihilistic could not care less about the threat of "flipping burgers" for life.

Moral agency refers to a kind of maturity, the capacity of a child to exercise virtue by making good decisions in his or her interests. Agency often requires a long-term view of the world cultivated from the wise counsel of parents, and other supportive adults and peers, who seek to direct children to the best long-term holistic health. Struggling adolescents making self-sabotaging decisions will almost certainly fail.

Regardless of race or class, education reform will succeed only if in tune with other needed reforms. Family, self-efficacy, and agency work in concert like one of Bach's Brandenburg concertos. Over one million annual reasons exist to stop playing rhetorical political games and ignoring the evidence, that educational success begins outside of the classroom.

SCHOOL FOR SCANDAL: HIP HOP GOES TO COLLEGE

Historically Black Colleges and Universities (HBCUs) have been the bedrock of black economic progress since 1837. Although America's 105 HBCUs represent only three percent of the nation's institutions of higher learning, they graduate nearly one-quarter of all blacks who earn undergraduate degrees. Among blacks, however, the virtues of a college education are under assault by the celebration of ignorance and misogyny codified in much of mainstream hip-hop. Thanks to a pathetic music video for the song "Rock Yo' Hips," from Crime Mob's newly released CD "Hated On Mostly," black colleges are being portrayed as nothing more than strip clubs and brothels.

Crime Mob's website alone should provoke massive protests on every HBCU campus in America. The mere juxtaposition of the words crime mob and college is outrageous. The naming of the group's mobile phone fan club, "Crime Mob College," and the creation of a misogynistic video to "Rock Yo Hips," set at a black college, provoke a real sense of despair. In the deplorable video, black college women dehumanize themselves while black men gawk and thrust at them. Black college cheerleaders dance like strippers, with lyrics linking them to "the pole," and the black men with metal-plated teeth in this video appear to be in need of something called "books."

The song is too revolting to quote at length but a few lyrics present a gross depiction:

"Look, lil' buddy/cute in the face/She rock her hips to the bass/She take a sip when she wave/And wanna get wit Lil'J/After she dance on that pole/I pull my cash so quick and fast."

Why did Warner Brothers film this sickening music video, obviously written and produced for the strip club market, on a black college campus? Does it mock black colleges and black people in general? Why do young people, whatever their color or race, enjoy watching blacks debase themselves? The hip-hop group Crime Mob "turns back the clock" on black progress more effectively than any repeal of affirmative action could ever do.

There are other reasons the "Rock Yo Hips" video is alarming. America's HBCUs are predominantly female (60 percent, or higher, on average) because of the absence of black men resulting from their 52 percent high school dropout rates, according to the most recent available national data compiled by Jay Greene of the Manhattan Institute. As 45 percent of all black students drop out of high school, compared to only 28 percent among Asians, there is a growing market that denigrates black women and views educated blacks as an absurd fantasy. Ignorant lyrics and animalistic sexuality set to music are what Americans are demanding and the music industry is happy to deliver. Americans of all races are sending a clear message: "We want music depicting black women as strippers and black men living as ignorantly as possible!"

Does this explain why there is such a devaluing of the black mind and dignity in much of today's hip-hop? Men who celebrate ignorance often encourage others to do the same.

Equally alarming is that black colleges seem not to care. Crime Mob's MySpace.com page lists an April 13 booking at South Carolina State University, a historically black college founded in 1890. Why would a black university whose population is predominantly female invite a group that celebrates ignorance and misogyny to their campus?

"Rock Yo Hips" continues to climb up the Billboard singles chart for the eighth straight week. With its recent appearance on MTV's Hip-Hop show "Sucka Free" and the group's begging its confused fans to vote the song onto MTV's "Total Request Live" (TRL), it appears likely that the world will have more opportunities to consume retrograde depictions of black people and American culture in general. Perhaps America needs a new civil rights movement—one that urges blacks not to mock their own educational opportunities and encourages American consumers to view all people in a more dignified light.

AMERICA'S 12TH GRADERS DUMBING DOWN IN SCIENCE

The 1994 comedy classic, *Dumb and Dumber*, spawned the catchphrase to describe American high school students' science aptitude performance. The Department of Education reports that science aptitude among high school seniors has declined during the past decade. America continues to graduate students who know less and less about the world because Americans, dominated by lust for material consumption and personal comfort, raise children lacking the education to make the world a better place.

In the American meritocracy, education is a means to a comfortable lifestyle, not a means of gaining knowledge to improve our world. Adults tell children to study so that they may personally escape poverty, rather than that they need an education to contribute to overall human flourishing. Grades—not preparation for a vocation directed at the good—are the bottom line for too many American parents.

The high school senior statistics came from the National Assessment of Education Progress (NAEP), a 2005 national comprehensive test administered by the Department of Education to more than 300,000 students in 50 states. The examination measured very basic knowledge of earth, physical, and life sciences and translated those scores into three achievement levels: advanced, proficient, and basic. The high school seniors' aptitude has declined sharply; only 54 percent performed at or above the basic level, compared with 57 percent in 1996. Eighteen percent performed at the proficient level, down from 1996 levels of 21 percent.

As expected, educators are scrambling to find the culprit to blame for the lower scores. In a *New York Times* story about the NAEP report, Assistant Secretary of Education Tom Luce said the declining science scores reflect a national shortage of fully qualified science teachers, especially in lower income areas, where physics and chemistry classes are often taught by teachers untrained in those subjects. "We have too few teachers with majors or minors in math and science," Mr. Luce said.

This confirms a now four-year-old prophecy issued by the National Research Council, part of the National Academy of Sciences, a prestigious group of U.S. scientists and engineers that offers advice to Congress and the government. The Council reported in 2002 that U.S. students continued to perform among the worst of all industrialized countries because schools have a critical shortage of qualified teachers in science, math and technology.

Some educators, of course, also blame low teacher salaries. However, a 2005 American Federation of Teachers report revealed that the average public school teacher's salary is $46,597, including average starting pay of $31,704. How is this low? Granted, these levels are not among the highest of all professions, but considering the summer vacation and the intrinsic reward of influencing the world's future, it is not a bad deal.

The problems are much deeper than salary. First, teaching is no longer a respected profession and the best and brightest citizens develop a social aversion to pursuing it. Many Americans continue to embrace the stupid adage that "those who can, do and those who can't, teach." If teachers cannot "cut it," then why do people continue to send their children to school? Why are the people in charge of equipping, forming, and shaping the hearts and minds of the world's future treated like Rodney Dangerfield—paid no respect?

Second, students are not encouraged to value learning about the world. Often students will say silly things such as, "Why do I need to learn physics? I can get a good job without it." Visionless parental pragmatists actually dissuade their children from taking courses that they do not "need" if there is no direct future financial benefit. How can one not "need" more knowledge about the world furnished by any legitimate area of intellectual inquiry?

This attitude only obscures the moral value of education. Ironically, a seemingly pragmatic obsession with financial reward also obscures education's economic value. In an ever-changing world, what appears to be a viable career today may disappear ten years hence. Students educated in a broad range of fundamental disciplines, including physics, can adapt more easily to the changing demands of a dynamic economy.

Concepts such as acceleration, Newton's three laws, coefficients of friction, centripetal force, and inductance benefit the life of the mind (as well as having practical applications for many careers).

Unless American culture refocuses on the value of education beyond material pragmatism, this society runs the risk of sabotaging an entire generation's ability to meet the future, unpredictable needs of a complex and broken world.

BACK TO SCHOOL, BACK TO PARENTS

As the school year kicks off, one does well to remember what really produces successful students: quality time spent with parents. This does not mean that parents show love only when their children earn high grades, nor does it mean that parents demand high grades at all costs. It means parents being dedicated to the welfare of their children and demonstrating by word and deed that they value education.

It is also important to note that, overall, children in loving, stable two-parent homes have an academic and social advantage over those who are not. Stressing this fact does not diminish in the least the achievements of single parents who strive to provide for their children to the best of their ability. It is no disrespect to such parents to emphasize that the ideal family situation is one in which both parents are present, and that it is this ideal that should guide individual decisions and commitments, social values, and public policy.

As evidence to back up this claim mounts, a new study by the Alabama Policy Institute demonstrates that most children in non-intact families are at an educational and social disadvantage compared to children from traditional families. The study, titled "Family Matters: Family Structure and Child Outcomes" and authored by three University of Chicago social scientists, explains the disadvantages of homes broken by divorce, cohabitation, and single-parenthood.

Empirical evidence confirms such findings. High achieving students were not always the most intelligent individuals in the class, but they usually came from homes where parents spent time giving moral guidance and academic support.

The study notes that, as early as age three, a child's ability to adapt to classroom routines appears to correlate with the marital situation of his parents. Among three and four year-olds, children with two biological parents in the home are three times less likely to experience emotional or behavioral problems than are those living in nontraditional households. Homes where mothers are cohabitating with fathers have particularly deleterious effects on pre-school age children, leading to a higher incidence of anxiety, depression, and behaviors of aggression and social withdrawal than children from traditional families.

Children whose parents read to them regularly enjoy substantial academic advantages when entering school, including higher learning aptitudes and reading skills. Since family structure affects the frequency of such activities, non-traditional arrangements place these children at a disadvantage.

The latest study simply amplifies a message already sounded by researchers. A 1996 report by the U.S. Department of Education claimed that fourth-graders in families with both biological parents scored higher on reading comprehension than students living in two-parent blended, single-mother, or other types of families. When income is a controlled variable, students in non-traditional homes still score below the mean of all students.

Among high school students, children from stepparent families were twice as likely to drop out of school. Children from "father-only" families were about 3 times likelier to drop out, and children from families headed by never-married women or "other-parent" families were 1.5 and 2 times more likely, respectively. Student whose parents divorce during the high-school years were 16 percent less likely to attend college than students from intact families.

Ancient wisdom prevails here again. Thousands of years ago, Moses told parents to journey daily, spending time with their children and teaching them what is best that they "may enjoy long life." When parents remain committed to loving each other and spending time with their children, the results are indisputable.

To increase student performance, both parents, whenever possible, must challenge and support their children to achieve scholastic excellence; more federal money, grade inflation, or social promotions are not the solutions. Parents must exercise self-sacrifice and the denial of immediate personal gratification. In other words, increasing student performance requires strong moral fiber. Without recognition of this moral link, educational progress for all students remains an unattainable ideal.

GRADING AMERICA'S GIVING:
GLOBAL ACTION WEEK FOR EDUCATION

Hundreds of thousands of activists, in 110 countries, are participating in Global Action Week for Education April 24–30. Oxfam, a prominent human rights advocacy organization, has unfortunately chosen to support the misleading "F" grade given to the United States by the Global Campaign for Education (GCE). Oxfam and the GCE are fooling the world into believing that America is not contributing significantly toward the goal of educating the 100 million children around the globe who are currently not in school. This apparent attempt at guilt manipulation is wrongheaded.

Providing training and formation for children is an obligation widely recognized among people of all religious and political persuasions. A child will be able to live in reasonable comfort only if he or she possesses the necessary tools to gain decent employment. Cultivation of the mind and moral instruction, moreover, regardless of their utilitarian value, speak to the deepest desires present in every human being.

To recognize this responsibility, however, is not necessarily to agree on a means to fulfill it. The United States received an "F" because its government is not giving 0.7 percent of its $2 trillion gross national income (GNI), to various countries and groups focusing on education. The 0.7 percent benchmark arbitrarily set by the World Bank also puts Japan, Germany, Italy, Spain, and Austria on the delinquent list.

GCE Bangladesh spokesperson Rasheda Chowdhury maintains that the US and the other G7 countries are "preventing children in poor countries from going to school" by not giving more money.

A more sophisticated assessment would recognize that the goal of better education demands the treatment of a host of interconnected issues, including the creation of stable communities.

The 2004 Copenhagen Consensus, a group of international environmental and humanitarian experts, have rightly noted that, given scarce resources, current global problems must be differentiated and prioritized, which is exactly what the US and the other G7 countries are doing. The experts' most important issues include controlling HIV/AIDS, providing nutrient rich diets, increasing international trade, controlling malaria, introducing new agricultural technologies, improving water supply and sanitation, and lowering the cost of starting new businesses by improving governance and fighting corruption.

These issues affect the vitality of education. In communities ravaged by HIV/AIDS, education cannot flourish. Providing more efficient and productive agricultural technologies is the best strategy for eradicating child labor needs. Nutritious diets and potable water provide a healthy platform for learning. The proliferation of free enterprise provides educated people a milieu in which they can use their knowledge and gifts to improve their communities. Lastly, children cannot learn and teachers cannot teach in the midst of violence and chaos.

Support for education, then, should not be isolated from the promotion of peace and stability.

During this week of distortions concerning Americans' lack of generosity, the facts provided in a recent report by Senator Jon Kyl (R-Arizona) bring the truth to light. Kyl reminds us that US government official development assistance (ODA) disbursements increased from $10 billion in 2000 to $19 billion in 2004. The US provided $2.4 billion for the global fight against AIDS in 2004.

The State Department reports that Americans privately give $34 billion in international philanthropy annually. Additionally, in 2004 alone, non-governmental funding from personal remittances, net private investment, and non-governmental organization grants totaled another $48 billion. Including these measures, since 1999 the United States has outpaced the entire European Union in giving as a percentage of GNI.

One should note that the US alone provides 22 percent of the U.N.'s budget ($362 million). In both 2003 and 2004, its government gave more than five times the amount of the European Commission to the World Food Program ($1 billion). Additionally, the US contributed $323 million to UNICEF (U.N. Children's Fund). In 2003, the US contributed $194 million to the U.N. Development Fund—15 percent of its budget.

Does America deserve an "F" from Oxfam? The objective answer is "no." The United States government will actually triple its aid to FTI education for fiscal 2005–6 to $400 million dollars. More importantly, American charity comprises a combination of governmental spending and private donations. An accurate assessment of aid to international education depends on a much broader definition than that used by critics, who mistakenly interpret "love thy neighbor" as the exclusive province of national governments.

MODERN MYTHS
ABOUT RACE AND SCHOOL PERFORMANCE

Fifty years after the Supreme Court's *Brown vs. Board of Education* ruling, the debate about race and academic performance still strays terribly far from the mark. The remarkable achievement of the Supreme Court ruling, which declared the legal segregation of public schools to be unconstitutional, set the foundation for equal opportunity. Today, the focus has shifted from equal opportunity to equal academic results and—even further from the point—to issues only indirectly related to schooling. Harvard's Civil Rights Project, for example, perceives freely chosen residential patterns in America as a basis for "resegregation" hysteria. When used to attack issues such as residential patterns, the real legacy of Brown is misunderstood.

The Brown decision guarantees that any student, regardless of his race, may attend a public school in his neighborhood. However, freedom to integrate may not result in the integration many had hoped for—as the failure of forced busing illustrates. In racially integrated neighborhoods, the neighborhood schools reflect the integration for those residents choosing public education. When neighborhood demographics change, or when parents choose other education options, public school demographics will change accordingly. This is a separate issue from legal racial segregation prohibited by Brown. The Harvard Project's 2004 study, "Brown at 50: King's Dream or Plessy's Nightmare?," falsely implies that *Brown vs. The Board of Education* aimed to "remedy" segregation in general. The ruling never intended to make an implicit, far more extensive, and ultimately impracticable requirement for universal integration of all neighborhoods. Residential segregation by choice is constitutional. If a neighborhood is voluntarily segregated, one should not lament that Americans are "turning back the clock."

Exaggerations concerning the desired results of racial integration, moreover, often rely on racially contrived data to gauge America's social progress. Misusing race in this way has led to widespread belief in several myths.

*Myth No. 1: Race is a helpful measure
of academic achievement disparities.*

Racial comparisons in education actually reveal very little. In addition, the achievement of white students taken as a group is not a very good standard. A more valuable analysis of American education draws comparisons to students in other developed countries. No race in America should represent the standard for evaluation because American students, collectively, lag behind students in other countries. For example, a 2003 Department of Education study found eighth-grade American students lagging behind Canadian, Russian, and Japanese students in math. They also trailed Canadian and Japanese students in science. The focus should be on raising academic performance for all American students, not just select racial and ethnic groups.

*Myth No. 2: Students at predominantly
minority schools cannot succeed.*

Thomas Sowell tells of an all black high school that, from 1870 to 1955, repeatedly equaled or exceeded national norms on standardized tests. During the entire 85-year history of Washington's M Street/Dunbar High School, most of its 12,000 graduates went on to higher education, an unusual achievement for any school—white or black—during this era. Some M Street/Dunbar School graduates attended Harvard and other elite colleges in the early twentieth century. Sowell reports, "As of 1916, there were nine black students, from the entire country, attending Amherst College. Six were from the M Street/Dunbar School. During the period from 1918 to 1923, graduates of this school went on to earn twenty-five degrees from Ivy League colleges, Amherst, Williams, and Wesleyan. The first blacks to graduate from West Point and Annapolis also came from this school. So did the first black full professor at a major university (Allison Davis at the University of Chicago). So did the first black federal judge, the first black general, the first black Cabinet member, the first black elected to the United States Senate since Reconstruction, and the discoverer of a method for storing blood plasma. During World War II, when black military officers were rare, there were more than two dozen graduates of M Street or Dunbar High School holding ranks ranging from major to brigadier general." Segregated schools also produced such notables as Mary McLeod Bethune, Thurgood Marshall, and Martin Luther King, Jr. The belief that racial diversity is a key to academic success has no empirical basis. If this myth were true, then it would be difficult to explain racial success in more mono-racial societies such as Japan, Germany, and the Netherlands. One study in San Diego found that Vietnamese and Asian immigrant children had a median grade point average 0.9 points higher than Mexican immigrants, and 0.8 points higher than students overall in San Diego. Membership in a racial minority does not cause sub-standard academic achievement.

Myth No. 3: Increased funding will remove the achievement gap between minority and white students.

Since 1980, the United States has increased federal education spending by 81 percent to the tune of $147.9 billion in fiscal year 2002, and the disparities continue. More money does not automatically lead to improved academic performance. If it did, American students would be among the highest achieving students in the world. Instead, America continues to lag behind Japan, Germany, and France in high school graduation rates. In Chicago, for example, 20 percent of public school students drop out before graduation.

Myth No. 4: Student performance has nothing to do with hard work.

Student achievement actually involves hard-working students and talented teachers. Students who work hard and enjoy intellectual challenge have the best chance of success. Perhaps this last myth is the most damaging of all. Hard work will cure many problems commonly attributed to a lack of funding or lack of diversity. Racial diversity, specifically the inclusion of white children does not result in minority students achieving more—intense studying every day does. God created human beings with an innate desire to learn and the potential to use acquired knowledge. The fostering of this God-given desire and potential leads to personal fulfillment and academic success.

In the final analysis, natural ability and a strong work ethic in both teachers and students are more relevant to student success than any other factors. Recognition of that fact would put the responsibility for achievement on individual students and teachers. Blaming the unquantifiable scapegoats of "race" and "class" would no longer be convenient in a climate of individual responsibility. Respect for the dignity of every student demands that educators, parents, and students themselves take an honest look at their efforts and judge how well they are fulfilling their own responsibilities.

MERIT-BASED STANDARDS IN EDUCATION: NOT FOR WHITES ONLY

On August 28, the nation marked the fortieth anniversary of Dr. Martin Luther King Jr.'s "I Have A Dream" speech. In it, Dr. King comments: "We can never be satisfied as long as our children are stripped and robbed of their dignity by signs stating 'for whites only.'" Unfortunately, forty years later, the Supreme Court again has institutionalized the second-class citizenship of African Americans with a strange twist on the old segregationist policy of reserving some privileges for "whites only." Only, this time around, the court seems to be saying that high standards in education are permissible only for white people. Jim Crow is alive and well in America's classrooms.

The University of Michigan affirmed this with the release of its new admissions policies on the anniversary of King's speech. The scant attention paid to what these policies say about the inherent dignity of minorities and the weaknesses in the applicant pool leaves many issues unresolved.

Simply stated, the argument for such policies rests on the unarticulated assumption that blacks and Hispanics cannot compete with whites on an equal playing field. Colleges and universities now have a two-tiered admissions process: one based on performance and human potentiality and the other based on presupposed inferiority. In contrast, the Christian tradition—which holds that all women and men are made in the image of God (Gen. 1:26–28)—opposes the idea that race and class make some inferior.

The image of God implies that every person possesses inherent worth and potentialities. Being made in God's image reveals that people have the capacity and desire to think, make choices, be creative, cultivate, work, build families, develop communities, and so on. A truly compassionate approach to injustice concerns itself with remedies that best provide for the full exercise and expression of human potentiality. *The Book of Common Prayer* contains a wonderful line thanking God for "setting us at tasks which demand our best efforts, and for leading us to accomplishments which satisfy and delight us."

Unfortunately, the current system substitutes racial identity for the demands of one's best efforts. Minorities fail to experience the delight and satisfaction of accomplishments achieved without preferential treatment because colleges and universities do not really expect these young people to succeed on their own merit. Instead, state-sanctioned racial discrimination continues to strip and rob minorities of their dignity. The incentive to work hard and take personal responsibility for one's performance applies to some and not others. Suspicion and stigma now accompany genuine achievement.

Colleges and universities draw from applicant pools; ultimately, the critical issue is the quality of the applicants. The systems and processes that feed the current applicant pool produce both well-equipped students and others that are competitively handicapped—irrespective of race and income. The good schools, therefore, have incentive to remain in the upper echelon, but the poor schools have no incentive to make radical improvements.

Parents aware of the problem are seeking options. Those who can afford it move to better school districts, home school, or seek private education. However, for many parents, options are constrained by third parties—such as the National Education Association (NEA) and its efforts to monopolize and usurp parental choice. As a power monopoly, the NEA has no interest in giving low-income parents the same type of choices that many NEA members themselves exercise with their own children. The NEA concerns itself with how parental choice programs "compete with funds" for state run schools. This insulting lobbying effort ignores the fact that low-income parents want quality education with proven results.

The system must emancipate low-income children shackled to failing schools. Granting the freedom to choose better schools is a step toward improving the future applicant pool for America's colleges and universities. Just because some parents are low-income does not mean they do not know and desire what is best for their children. Low-income parents, as God's image bearers, deserve the dignity, respect, freedom, and power to make choices about where their children will be educated. Do not all Americans deserve to enjoy the same freedoms, or is educational choice to be exercised by "whites only" (or, more precisely, by high-income Americans only)?

Every year one sees the results of a primary and secondary education process in need of repair as colleges artificially manipulate the results of the current system to create the impression of a system one wished existed. This approach will never succeed. A system that constrains human potential with mediocre standards, racial discrimination, no accountability, and inhibited parental choice, forces colleges to resort to the dehumanizing two-tiered admissions process.

If the results of America's education system are undesirable, maybe radical changes in the system are necessary. America needs a primary and secondary education process that produces a multi-racial critical mass of well-educated students who respond to intellectual challenge by giving their best efforts. America needs a process that produces an ethnically diverse body of students to unlock human potentiality. America needs a process by which all students enjoy equal opportunities to discover their God given talents and gifts. America needs a process that allows people to experience the blessing of failure. America needs a process by which hard work earns rewards for all and not penalties for some. America needs a process in which all parents escape surrogate education decision makers. Finally, this country needs a process whereby no child is stripped and robbed of dignity by a system that demands high standards for "whites only."

HARVARD'S CIVIL RIGHTS PROJECT MISSES THE MARK

The Civil Rights Project at Harvard University just released a report noting that government sponsored desegregation programs are failing. The authors note that many of America's largest metropolitan districts have "resegregated." This is not surprising.

Unfortunately, the authors also intimate that a possible (and probable) reason for this is the dismantling of several desegregation plans in school districts across America. That is, schools are resegregating because government is not using its power to achieve racial integration. This raises important concerns.

First, *Brown vs. the Board of Education* prohibited districts from using race to prevent children from attending schools in their own district. Remember, a school in Linda Brown's district denied her admittance because of race.

Today, schools deny admission to no ethnic minorities based on their race. The law was a success. What the Harvard study suggests is that it is wrong for schools to reflect the racial demography of their respective communities.

Segregated public schools exist because Americans, largely choose to live in segregated communities. They make this choice because they want to, not because they have to. For example, middle and upper class African Americans, because of choice—not housing discrimination—dominate the Cascade section of southwest Atlanta. The number of whites in a given school declines because white families move to other areas.

The study does note in one phrase that community public schools "reflect the segregation that exists in housing throughout metropolitan areas." Since this is true why, then, did this not govern the analysis of the data? When communities are integrated, community school bodies will reflect this integration.

Second, why must community schools integrate? The study notes that interracial exposure has positive implications for white socialization and minority academic performance. There is, unfortunately, no data to support this claim.

Do African Americans and Latinos need to be around white students in order to learn and perform well? African American and Latino teachers, administrators, and parents should be insulted at the idea that minority students need "exposure" to white children and teachers in order to increase academic performance.

Many brilliant African Americans and Latinos have been educated in racially isolated environments without negative academic consequences. In the past, barriers occurred when discrimination based on race prevented educated minorities from making use of their education.

Are white children somehow better socialized just because they have been exposed to African Americans and Latinos occupying the same space in a building? Again, there is no evidence at all to support the idea that "exposure" results in better socialization and changing of attitudes. One may be "exposed" to healthy food once a week in the grocery store but it does not change what he eats.

Third, discrimination, not segregation, is the evil in this equation. Treating people based on their race is unconstitutional. In Lynn, Massachusetts, there is a court case pending because a public school denied a white girl admittance because of racial imbalance. That is, the school had too many white students already! This scenario would be unlikely, to say the least, if the child were Latino and the school denied her admission because it had fulfilled its Latino quota. Imagine!

If community public schools are receptive to admitting all community area students, then there is no need to force integration by race or class. If illegal discrimination does not exist, there is no need for government intervention.

It is not the responsibility of the government to determine where certain races should live. Nor is it the government's responsibility to determine where certain races should attend school. It is not the responsibility of the government to force people to integrate their social lives either.

If minority parents want their children to attend a better school, there are two options: (1) they can move to a good school district or (2) they can demand quality from their children's current school. Relocating is a real possibility. For those who do not want to move, their responsibility as a taxpayer and parent is to demand excellence in their community's schools.

Fourth, the study is reductionist and simplistic in its analysis. Americans are no longer divided simply by race. African American, Latino, and Asian college graduates do not always live in their respective ethnic communities. The study confuses a racial phenomenon with one associated essentially with class. Most American communities are divided by income level and many other factors.

Racial desegregation plans are one-dimensional, unnecessary, and doomed to failure. State run desegregation plans will not achieve social integration. Since the study looks only at race, it is stating only one variable in a complex equation. As such, one learns the earth shattering fact that ethnic minorities live near each other. This is not a breakthrough study.

What the Harvard study fails to understand is that true social integration in American communities can occur only when people recognize each other as image bearers of God. The image of God transcends race and class. Therefore, if one sees his neighbor first as an image bearer of God, he is more likely to treat that person with dignity and respect.

American communities and, by extension, American public schools experience segregation because people assign value to the human person based on superficial features, such as race and class. Many people distort the image of God to conform to their own likeness. This results in limiting relationships and community preference to people like themselves. People live, worship, play, and so on with people who look and think the same as they do. Until this narrow perspective changes, any efforts at integration will be simply cosmetic and unfortunately, as the study demonstrates, temporary.

Subject/Name Index